DEAF
EMPOWERMENT

DEAF EMPOWERMENT

Emergence, Struggle, and Rhetoric

Katherine A. Jankowski

Gallaudet University Press
Washington, D.C.

Photographs on pages 25, 27, 126, 128, 129, and 130 courtesy of Galluadet University Archives. Photograph on page 60 by Chun Louie. Still frames on page 61 taken from *Preservation of the Sign Language,* courtesy of Gallaudet University Archives.

Gallaudet University Press
Washington, D.C. 20002

07 05 03 01   6 5 4 3

Library of Congress Cataloging-in-Publication Data

Jankowski, Katherine A..
    Deaf empowerment : emergence, struggle, and rhetoric / Katherine A. Jankowski.
       p.   cm.
    Includes bibliographical references and index.
    ISBN 1-56368-061-0
    1. Deaf—United States—History.   2. Deaf—Civil rights—United States—History.
    3. Deaf—Means of communication—United States—History. I. Title.
    HV2530.J35   1997
    362.4'2'0973—dc21   97-11897
                                                                          CIP

Interior design by Dennis Anderson

Sign illustrations by Paul M. Setzer
Sign language model, Catherine Langerman
Composition by Wilsted & Taylor Publishing Services

Contents

Preface

Much can be learned about a group of people and the power structure of their society by studying the process of change and its impact on the greater society. My first experience with attempting to alter the status quo occurred when I was thirteen years old. My classmates and I arrived at the conclusion that we were not being challenged to our fullest potential and, therefore, were being cheated out of our education. I personally led a student protest in the classroom, complete with picket signs. Although this humble protest hardly made a dent in our society, it taught me about democracy and equal rights.

My interest in social change and my desire to salute the efforts of the Deaf community—past, present, and future—created the impetus for my dissertation study, on which this book is based. *Deaf Empowerment: Emergence, Struggle, and Rhetoric* is intended to illustrate how hard-fought struggles by our ancestors helped pave the way for the unprecedented Deaf President Now protest of 1988, which in turn, continues to empower the Deaf community in so many valuable ways. Our society is a much better place because of these efforts.

This book is also about communication. It offers a unique perspective of communication not only as the means of conveying information but also as the central issue of the Deaf movement, thus, making this a reflexive study of communication. This approach made the book more personal for me. I chose to study communication because I grew up in a community where communication was not taken for granted. I lived in the Deaf community and saw the ease with which Deaf people congregated and communicated in our beautiful language of signs. Paradoxically, for the first one-and-a-half years of my academic life I attended a day school for deaf children where sign language was prohibited. I then attended public schools for most of my remaining school years, a time when interpreters were virtually unheard of. These experiences taught me to value communication both as an issue and as the means to effective interaction. It seems fitting, therefore, that I have chosen to make this a study on communication about communication.

The Deaf community is a truly unique cultural entity—one that I am proud to be a member of. My hope is that readers will gain insights into and new respect for the struggles and achievements of this most fascinating community.

1

Introduction

Electricity filled the air on March 6, 1988, as large crowds flocked to the auditorium at Gallaudet University, the world's only liberal arts university for Deaf[1] students, to await the announcement of the name of Gallaudet's first Deaf president. The Deaf community[2] had worked feverishly for this moment. Letters, calls, and telegrams had been sent to the Gallaudet board of trustees, as well as to senators and representatives, to urge the selection of a Deaf candidate. A preselection rally held on the campus had built up the momentum.

Expectations were very high. For many, it was a foregone conclusion that Gallaudet's next president would be Deaf. Surely, after 124 years, the community would have its first Deaf president. Of the three finalists, two were Deaf Gallaudet alumni. But excitement quickly turned to shock and anger when, instead of a formal announcement, a press release was distributed announcing the selection of a hearing person, Elisabeth Ann Zinser, vice chancellor of the University of North Carolina at Greensboro, as the new president.

The angry crowd immediately marched to the hotel where board members were meeting, and for an entire week the students and their supporters closed down the campus. During the protest, the students compiled a list of four demands, including the resignation of Zinser and her replacement with a Deaf president; the resignation of Jane Bassett Spilman, chair of the board of trustees; the restructuring of the board with a 51 percent Deaf majority (at the time, only four of its twenty-one members were Deaf);

1

and finally, an agreement that there be no reprisals against protest participants. The conflict between the students, who demanded a Deaf president, and Zinser and Spilman, who were not willing to give in to these demands, was played up extensively by the media. The protests made front-page news all over the country, and national television as well.

This scenario describes a phenomenon known as a "social movement." Similar accounts could describe many other movements, now a familiar part of contemporary life. Social movements, many believe, are necessary to achieve the American dream of equality, and in struggles for democracy elsewhere. Indeed, without social movements, Americans would still be under English rule, African Americans would not be recognized as full-fledged citizens with voting rights, women's roles would still be primarily in the home, and young children would still be working under horrendous conditions, as would older workers.

There is, however, much more to social movements than just a struggle for equality or democracy. Social movements generally represent a nondominant group and its intention to change the existing social order. Thus, social movements are often a threat to the dominant group and are essentially a struggle for the redistribution of power.

Social movements acquire power as they translate their ideology into action on behalf of the cause of the group. The ideology of the social movement is communicated through rhetoric. *Rhetoric,* as used here, refers to any communicative act that influences thought and behavior. As such, rhetoric includes both language and nonlinguistic symbols such as clothing, pictures, advertisements, performances, and any other emblems. Rhetoric creates and sustains the ideology and counterideology proposed by both the dominant culture and the social movement. The Gallaudet protest, for instance, is an example of an ideological conflict. The board of trustees felt that administrative skills were far more important than linguistic and cultural considerations, and this view manifested itself in their choice of a hearing candidate. The Deaf community had a considerably different view, which prompted the protest. This struggle between the board of trustees and the Deaf community represented ideological differences, and this conflict became a social reality through the rhetoric presented during the week-long protest.

Language shapes, as well as illustrates, social reality. A group's language transmits its ideology, consciously and unconsciously. A rhetorical inquiry, for example, shows how differing meanings of the word *Deaf* serve the ideological force of the two sides confronting each other in the Gallaudet protest. Further, language can create and sustain power. A social movement that transforms ideology into rhetoric has the potential to acquire power. This process of acquiring power transforms feelings of powerlessness into feelings of empowerment. Of interest here is how empowerment is achieved through language. More specifically, how has rhetoric shaped the empowerment of the cultural identity of the Deaf social movement?

Ideology in Social Movements

Inherent in any dominant culture or organized entity is a philosophy or set of beliefs that serves as the dominant ideology. Through rhetoric, which brings the dominant ideology into everyday life, people construct their reality of the world, their sense of themselves, their identities, and their relationships to other people and to society (Fiske 1987). People literally talk their way through life, translating their beliefs into action through such talk (Burke [1941] 1973). The rhetoric of the dominant group frames justification for day-to-day action, thus enforcing norms that keep subordinates in line and maintain the status quo. The rhetorical process that produces this conformity to norms is so pervasive because it is so often overlooked as a basis for the power of the dominant group (Foucault 1980). Even when subordinates acknowledge that dominant discourses impose upon them behaviors that they loath, they may continue to conform to the norm for a number of reasons. Sociologists Peter Berger and Thomas Luckmann offer one explanation, that of habitualization. People are creatures of habit and perform practices automatically without questioning the process (1966). Another reason may be the fear of rejecting the status quo and having to face the heightened responsibility that comes with independence (Freire 1970). Dominant practices are by no means a simple process of domination and subordination. While the ongoing discourse enables the dominant culture to continue to secure the consent of the marginalized group, this consent is not always easily granted. Through rhetoric, opposing ideologies continuously challenge the dominant discourse, transforming the dominant ideology in a complex, constantly changing process.

One channel for this rhetorical conflict is the social movement. Movements, and the social change they induce, are created through rhetorical processes of confrontation and challenge. Societies control behavior through rhetorical constructions of particular patterns of thinking and acting that sustain the accomplishment of normality. Movements challenge that normality. In the process, they provide their members with an alternative rhetoric that brings a different ideology, different behaviors, and different identity into day-to-day life. The women's movement is a case in point.[3] In the early history of the women's movement, women adopted the rhetoric of "all men are created equal." This movement began with the women active in the abolition movement.[4] These women were living on the platform, attaining a status through which women's voices were heard as clearly as men's. Several women, most notably the feminist activist sisters Angelina and Sarah Grimke, began to expand on that rhetoric to include the emancipation of women (Japp 1985). In the beginning, not all women working for the abolition of slavery endorsed this position. Eventually, however, the rhetoric of "equality for all" empowered increasing numbers of women and paved the way toward women's suffrage. With the advent of women's suffrage, the movement grew, and new discourses emerged. Consequently, the women's movement encountered a variety of rhetorical conflicts. One such conflict was the struggle for the rhetoric of "personhood" versus that of "womanhood" (Campbell 1983).

Those taking the stance of personhood argued that men and women are equal, while those advocating womanhood stressed the differences between women and men.

The women's movement is much more complicated than the above discussion suggests, but it serves to illustrate the role of rhetoric in empowering marginalized groups. The rhetoric of the women's movement also distinguishes it from the patriarchal society and from other movements that emerge from a different discourse. Even within today's women's movement, distinctive groups embody differing ideologies through their rhetoric—for example, Marxist feminists, radical feminists, and lesbian feminists.[5]

Through rhetoric, social movements create internal and external social tensions. Some members of the movement may demand total preservation of its ideology, while others will want to modify positions in order to attract more borderline members or to effect change from within the dominant structure. When the rhetoric of movement leaders focuses on the purification of group ideology, greater cohesiveness within the group may take place, but this may risk widening the gap between the movement and the dominant culture (Conrad 1981). On the other hand, by adapting their rhetoric to please others or to increase potential for making changes, social movements risk creating internal strife. When rhetoric becomes "less visionary," the base for holding the group together crumbles (285).

An important feature of social movement discourse is its consciousness-raising potential. Raising the consciousness of formerly apathetic or ignorant members or outsiders often creates social unrest. "Raising the consciousness" refers to the process of removing the power of discourse to direct habitual actions. Suddenly members frame formerly habitual actions in ways that offer choice. Such rhetorical strategies have the potential to open up people's minds to new ideas and more radical solutions (Wilson 1973). Consciousness raising is an important aspect of empowering individuals in social movements. The interaction between rhetorical strategies of the movement and the emerging sense of self-worth in consciousness raising marks the emergence of a discourse of empowerment. Now empowered with a rhetoric that brings a different ideology to day-to-day life, the oppressed have a new power to celebrate their heritage, to reject labels imposed on them by their oppressors, and to acquire new traits that enhance feelings of pride and power (Stewart, Smith, and Denton 1989).

Empowerment in Social Movements

The term *empowerment* is so widely used that it is often given a variety of interpretations and thus merits explanation. Definitions for *empowerment* have included upward mobility, self-assertion, and political activity. Writers Ann Bookman and Sandra Morgen explain that empowerment "begins when they [marginalized members] change their ideas about the causes of their powerlessness, when they recognize the systematic forces that oppress them, and when they act to change the condition of their lives" (Bookman and Morgen 1988, 4). Bookman and Morgen conclude that "fundamentally, then, empowerment is a process aimed at consolidating, maintaining, or changing the nature and distribution of power in a particular cultural context" (4). This process, however, includes much resistance and consent along the way as the sources of power come into conflict. This book will treat empowerment as a process through which a marginalized group alters the distribution of power between itself and the dominant culture.

Even though *empowerment* is currently a fashionable term, not much is known about the place of empowerment in social movements. This seems surprising in view of the inherent nature of social movements. Social movements, after all, generally come into existence to alter power relationships between people or between people and the dominant structure. A social movement often emerges when members come together after realizing a desire to stop their oppressors from continuing to control them, to paternalize them, or to oppress them.

The notion of marginalized people becoming empowered by joining a social movement and in particular identifying with a specific ideology makes sense when considering the status of most marginalized groups. Marginalized people in general do not have much power over their destinies because they are often not represented in decision making or policy making, even when it directly affects members of their culture (Kramarae 1981). They are often denied access to the dominant culture in such matters because their discourse is not valued. Many marginalized people find their experiences interpreted for them by those in the dominant culture who control the discourse in which the interpretation proceeds (Schulz 1984). As a result, because their discourse and experiences have so long been devalued and denigrated, it is difficult to overcome the disbelief that their experiences are indeed valid and legitimate. In order to develop the "courage to be and to speak," it is often necessary to build up a strong sense of identity within the marginalized group (Daly 1978, 264). This is empowerment.

The Deaf Social Movement

In examining the role of rhetoric as it shapes empowerment, we turn to the specific cultural group under study—the Deaf social movement, its character, and its struggles over the issue of communication. The Gallaudet protest, for instance, illustrates the surfacing of Deaf ideology in a rhetorical process of empowerment. After years of exclusion from decision-making policies made primarily by hearing people, including the selection of a hearing president at Gallaudet, the Deaf movement asserted its identity to attain access to power.

Like other marginalized groups, Deaf people have often found that their opinions are neither valued nor encouraged in decisions affecting their welfare. As a result, the tendency of many Deaf people has been to stay out of the public sphere, even when their own fates are being debated. However, some Deaf people have not been willing to grant the dominant society permission to dominate them. These Deaf people find that their beliefs are at odds with the dominant culture, and they want to reject the dominant perception of them, to create a new language with which to describe themselves. Thus emerges the birth of the Deaf social movement with a rhetoric that contrasted with that of the social order. Even though the rhetoric of the Deaf social movement has shifted over the years, the prevailing theme has centered around communication as subject matter as well as vehicle.

In the dominant culture, in which speech is the primary mode of communication, it is almost impossible to imagine communicating without speech. It is even more difficult to imagine anyone rejecting speech as a mode of communication. Many members of the dominant society remain oblivious, until enlightened, to the fact that there is indeed a group of people in this world who use speech only occasionally or not at all. Yet, the Deaf cultural community constitutes such a group. In this community, communication is not taken for granted. In fact, communication is so highly valued that it is at the core of the conflict between the Deaf community and the dominant society.

Historically, Deaf people have fought against hearing professionals who educate Deaf children in the oral modality (a reference to the phenomenon of "oralism," which encompasses the use of primarily spoken speech and speechreading to communicate), using sign language only as a last resort, if at all. This philosophy is based on the belief that speech is the most valuable educational attainment for Deaf children. Inherent in this belief is the notion that Deaf people should become as much like hearing people as possible. Deaf children should become adults who are able to "integrate" into mainstream society. What better way is there to do this than by enforcing the values of speech, the English language, along with the cultural norms of hearing society?

A by-product of this "integration" mentality is evident in the increasing numbers of Deaf children in mainstream programs (an all-encompassing term for a variety of programs, including small classrooms of Deaf students in public schools, and Deaf students placed in public school classrooms, with or without interpreters) and the diminishing numbers of Deaf children in residential schools. In fact, such strategies isolate an increasing number of Deaf children from other Deaf children and teach them that the best way to achieve success is to acquire communication skills that are most acceptable to the dominant society. This argument appears convincing to many hearing and Deaf people.

To culturally Deaf people, as well as supporters of cultural pluralism, however, the goal of "integration" leaves much to be desired. Those sharing this ideology believe that "integration" works in theory more than in practice. They point to the frustrations of Deaf people in attempting to achieve even minimal speaking ability; to the years of focusing primarily on acquiring speech skills at the expense of receiving an education; to struggling with the English language because they are not taught in a visual mode, nor in a language that most benefits their visual orientation; and to devalued self-esteem because they are not taught to take pride in their cultural heritage.[6]

Supporters of Deaf cultural preservation face much resistance to their ideology. Those who favor "integration" believe that American Sign Language (ASL) and Deaf cultural norms are detrimental to the acquisition of English language skills and ultimately serve as a barrier to successful employment and subsequent promotion.[7] They also believe that political decisions should reflect integrative goals as well. Proponents of Deaf culture believe that the mainstream advocates are selling the Deaf community out and that the way to achieve power is to maintain that Deaf people are indeed a unique cultural entity that should be perceived as a diverse element in an already diverse American society.[8] Political decisions should also reflect the unique needs of the Deaf community and not attempt to categorize Deaf people with other groups who do not face similar issues.

This struggle within the Deaf social movement is not unique and is analogous to other movement struggles. A similar comparison is reported by Robert L. Scott and Wayne Brockriede in their rhetorical analysis of the Black Power movement (1969). They describe the dilemma of African Americans in a situation where they may be viewed as tokens or as radicals. Those who become tokens are demeaned as hypocritical. If tokenism is only the first step toward eventual negotiation, the token is viewed by society as ungrateful. However, the person who rejects tokenism is perceived as a troublemaker. Many Black Power proponents argue that it is only when they unite as a group apart from the dominant culture that they can begin to make their power felt, and that this power will work for improved conditions.

Although this rhetorical dilemma is not unique to the Deaf social movement, what makes the Deaf movement unique is that the struggle centers on the fundamental right to communicate. Unlike other marginalized group members who declare loudly their demand to be heard in a modality shared by the dominant society, Deaf Americans are excluded from communicating their demands in that dominant mode of speech. As the dominant ideology has not yet fully accepted the notion of sign communication, the right to communicate in this way has long been sought by culturally Deaf people. This right, central to the ideology of the Deaf social movement, will be the focus of this book.

A Note on Method

A study of the way in which rhetoric shapes empowerment for the Deaf social movement must incorporate the theoretical precepts of ideological analysis and empowerment delineated earlier, with a specific focus on the cultural Deaf community. This means giving specific attention to the rhetorical strategies that empower the Deaf social movement as its members counter the contrasting dominant ideology. The following questions guide this study: How does the Deaf social movement define the dominant rhetoric that marginalizes it? How does the Deaf social movement strategically posture the conflict involved in this difference in rhetoric? How does the rhetoric through which the Deaf cultural community counters the dominant social discourse empower the Deaf cultural community?

This type of examination suggests a need for the use of methodologies that can examine rhetoric from the perspective of dominance and resistance. For this reason, a rhetorical analysis based on a combination of several methodologies guides this study. This combination incorporates the principles of historical analysis, the ethnography of communication, and Foucaultian analysis.

For this rhetorical analysis, three stages comprise the procedure for this study. First, the rhetoric to be examined in this study is defined. The next procedure is to analyze and interpret the rhetorical acts operating within the ideological struggle between the dominant and the dominated, with particular focus on the rhetorical strategies of the dominated as they strive to empower their community. Finally, theory and action are merged to understand the contribution of these findings to the discipline of communication.

Defining the Rhetoric

The first procedure for the rhetorical study of the Deaf movement was to define the rhetoric to be examined. Primarily, I was interested in the movement's counter-rhetoric created in response to the dominant culture's enforcement of "normality." Since the time period of this study covered nearly a century, the methods for collecting relevant rhetoric depended on two types of research: a historical examination and an ethnography of communication.

For the chapters covering primarily the historical movement, I relied on surviving historical artifacts. Although the Deaf culture is predominantly maintained through a visual channel, published documents comprise much of the data for this study. In this historical examination, rhetorical acts that illustrated the tensions of the Deaf social movement's resistance to the dominant ideology were noted and documented. To limit the scope of this examination, only rhetorical acts that pertained to the theme of preservation of Deaf culture were the focus.

For more contemporary and directly observable phenomena, it was possible to visit the site of events to get a firsthand account. An approach such as the ethnography of communication, which refers to the description and analysis of specific cultural communicative behaviors, is especially useful for the study of the Deaf social movement because it takes into account the visual nature of communication for the Deaf community.[9]

The first step for most ethnographers or participant-observers is to clarify their role in the community under study (Trenholm 1991). Some researchers may choose not to reveal their research intent in order to become full-fledged participants. Others may prefer to make clear their purpose, which then gives them permission to query participants in the community. As a Deaf person, I have ready access to the Deaf community, and my presence at various events is not questioned. Collection of data was, then, made with relative ease. In addition, when I needed to clarify my role in order to videotape events or ask further questions, my being an "insider" proved advantageous in that my peers were willing to comply.

The second step of ethnography is to make and record observations (Trenholm 1991). As there is no written form of ASL, it has been necessary to either document ideas and themes of rhetorical acts in written English or to videotape events. These methods are far from perfect, but they come closer to capturing the communicative intent of the rhetorical act. Even with videotaped phenomena, which most closely resembled the original event, translations had to be made for the purpose of this study. Translations proved difficult because of the need to translate from one language to another. At most, this resulted in translations that do not capture the full essence of rhetorical acts, but rather, present a moderately equivalent depiction.

The final step of ethnography is to analyze and interpret the collected data according to the questions guiding the analysis of the rhetoric of the Deaf social movement. As a case in point, the Gallaudet protest, in addition to an examination of publications, required the use of ethnographic strategies. From television, I taped approximately twenty-five hours' worth of the nightly news and documentaries, all covering the week-long protest. Other sources included posters, artwork, and slogans available from the Gallaudet archives and the Smithsonian Institution, as well as my personal observations. In other cases, data was collected through participant observation at a number of events. I attended and videotaped public addresses at various rallies and public gatherings, as well as other symbolic expressions decrying the status quo. These symbolic expressions included ASL poetry, works of art, and theatrical productions that further illuminated the Deaf experience.

Examination of Rhetorical Acts

The second step of the rhetorical analysis was to examine the rhetorical forces operating within the ideological struggle between the dominant and dominated, with particular attention to the strategies used by the dominated to empower their community. The writings of Michel Foucault, a theorist whose works often centered on discourse and power, were particularly helpful in this regard, especially in his conception of culture.

According to Foucault, "normality" is a rhetorical construct (1970). The normal person is only a vision created by what Foucault calls "the human sciences." Foucault's position here is instrumental to the study at hand, as it is the dominant culture's notion of the "normal" person that contrasts with the ideology of the Deaf social movement. The resistance movement of the Deaf community is also most often directed at Foucault's characterization of the human sciences. The human sciences encompass authorities representing social institutions, such as educators, administrators, medical personnel, and those from the helping professions.

Through rhetoric, these authorities legitimize the "normal person," leaving out countless groups of people, including Deaf people, who deviate from the norm. These authorities thus pave the way for a society that "legitimately regulates its population and seeks out signs of disease, disturbance and deviation so that they can be treated and returned to normal functioning under the watchful eyes of one or other policing system" (Philp 1985, 75–76). The inherent nature of social movements is that they typically resist the cultural ideals of the "normal person," and such is the case for the Deaf social movement. This book focuses on the resistance of the Deaf social movement to the human sciences and their interest in "normalizing" the Deaf person. Foucault's genealogical method corresponds to the study of such resistance, as it is an examination of the rhetoric of empowerment performed by those "who resist the subjugating effects of power: those who, like some feminists [and culturally Deaf people], refuse to surrender their bodies to the established practices of medicine [including the pathological sciences so prevalent in the Deaf community] . . . and those who resist the identities imposed upon them by others" (Philp 1985, 76).

In using Foucaultian analysis, I have taken the following approach. The first step was to study the recurrent themes as they pertained to the ideological struggle between the Deaf community and the dominant society. I have found that these themes center around issues of communication with the educational institution as the primary battleground throughout the history of the Deaf movement. Even though the dominant ideology will not be the focus of this rhetorical analysis, it provides the context in response to which resistance rhetoric was developed. In addition, this step focuses on the dominant perception of Deaf people, thus highlighting the oppressive forces Deaf people were dealing with prior to and during the emergence of the Deaf social movement.

My second step was to examine the various rhetorical strategies and their empowering functions. This part of the process focused on rhetorical acts from a number of individuals and groups spanning the past one hundred or so years, revealing the tensions centering around communication and cultural preservation, with a particular emphasis on how the Deaf social movement used these rhetorical strategies to empower its community.

The Findings

The final step of this rhetorical study was to merge theory and action with a conscious effort toward effecting social change (Littlejohn 1989). In rhetorical theory, this involves moving beyond an interpretation of the rhetoric under study toward making a contribution to the field of communication. This is conducted by evaluating whether the rhetoric studied appears to correspond to existing knowledge of rhetorical functions or whether it suggests a new explanation (Foss 1989).

Two caveats help locate this study. First, it is necessary to note that, although this study used methods created primarily for oral and written modalities, the treatment of these methods in this study incorporated the language, culture, and experiences of Deaf people. Historically, rhetorical criticism has been formulated largely in the context of hearing people. This has led to the assumption that all communication is primarily oral or written. Deaf people, however, perceive the world differently from hearing people (Padden and Humphries 1988; Sacks 1989). The world view of Deaf people is based on vision, rather than on hearing. This visual orientation is so pervasive that it not only represents how Deaf people see the world, but is a factor in how Deaf people acquire language, how they process thought, and how they communicate. These factors have evolved into a Deaf culture in which a different mode of communication has created a language and a lifestyle.

In addition, the perceptions, values, and experiences of Deaf people are not incorporated into the dominant language. The field of communication is a case in point. Numerous communications departments, textbooks, and even the national organization (the Speech Communication Association) define communication as "speech," and when communication departs from the norm, it is labeled a "communication disorder."

Because of this perceived "deviation from the norm," the communication and language of Deaf people are devalued and denigrated. Educators of Deaf students often equate "language" with English, overlooking the fact that American Sign Language is a language as well. These educators express their concept of communication similarly in statements like "Deaf kids can't communicate" (Snyder 1988, 8). Such statements are overly dramatic and grossly misleading. A more appropriate statement would illustrate that many Deaf people do not rely on speech as a primary mode of communication.

The second caveat relates to translations made from American Sign Language to English. Most rhetorical texts critiqued in the communication discipline are more easily decoded into a written language than is ASL. Although the rhetoric of the Deaf social movement includes printed documents in English, much of the rhetoric is generated in American Sign Language, and thus, requires translation.

Organization of the Study

The first chapter introduces the nature of the study, its theoretical foundations, and delineates the method that guides the study. The second chapter presents a historical overview of the Deaf cultural community. Such a review presents the background of the Deaf social movement and helps the reader understand the rhetorical process that guides the movement.

The heart of the study begins with Chapter 3, which examines the rhetorical conflict as the dominant society attempts to "normalize" the Deaf person. The historical efforts by the dominant culture to enforce the mode of speaking and speechreading on Deaf people and their resistance to these efforts are highlighted. Chapter 4 moves on to the 1960s and 1970s, during which the liberating movements came to the fore and presented a new context for the Deaf social movement. Specifically, this chapter addresses strategies to establish sign language as a respected modality and language, and to condemn the social-engineering practices of the dominant culture. Chapter 5 brings us to the most effective protest conducted by the Deaf social movement—the Gallaudet University uprising.

Chapter 6 moves on to the aftermath of the Gallaudet protest and the ensuing strategies of the Deaf cultural movement. This more recent movement reveals a trend similar to diversity movements in its vision of a multicultural society. The multicultural framework that guides these movements suggests three necessary attributes for community building: creating a sense of self-worth, building an internal foundation for community building, and full participation in the public sphere. Chapter 7, the concluding chapter, addresses the contribution of this study to the body of research on social movements, discusses the strategies of the Deaf movement, and evaluates whether these strategies can lead to a multicultural society. Further, a fourth attribute for community building is suggested: a discourse of "humanitarianism."

Notes

1. Recent custom has been to distinguish between the audiological and cultural representation of "deaf" people by using the lowercase "d" to refer to the audiological condition of "hearing loss" and the capital "D" to refer to a community of people who share a language—American Sign Language—and a culture. This book will adopt that convention as well.

2. The phrase *Deaf community*, as used in this book, generally refers to Deaf people in the United States who use American Sign Language and share cultural values, traditions, and interactive patterns.

3. For more information on historical accounts of the women's movement, see Banner 1980; Gurko 1976; Hymowitz and Weissman 1978; O'Neill 1971; and Smith 1970. A comprehensive rhetorical treatment of early women speakers can be found in Campbell 1989. Other rhetorical contributions include Campbell 1983 and 1986; Conrad 1981; Japp 1985; Smith-Rosenberg 1975; and Solomon 1988.

4. Scholars have traditionally placed the women's movement as having taken root in the abolition movement. The premise has been that women in the abolition movement were treated shabbily by their male counterparts, thus creating the impetus for the women's movement. More recent research has pointed out, however, that rhetorical scholars reached such conclusions from the perspective of the male-dominated sphere (Carlson 1992). This has led to a focus on women who spoke to audiences composed of both men and women in their attempts to persuade men to work for change, while ignoring studies of women who refused to speak to such audiences and who spoke only to female audiences. As recent research indicates, the study of women who spoke only to female audiences reveals factors of oppression and consciousness that challenge traditional arguments. Consequently, the perception that the abolition movement paved the way for the women's movement may not be totally accurate.

5. For general discussions of distinctive feminist ideologies, see Donovan 1985; Elshtain 1981; Hawkesworth 1990; and Jaggar and Rothenberg 1978.

6. Deaf people perceive the world differently from hearing people because their orientation is based on the visual rather than the aural (e.g., Padden and Humphries 1988; Sacks 1989).

7. For such perspectives on mainstreaming, see Reich, Hambleton, and Houldin 1977; and Ross 1978 and 1990. Ross, for instance, argues that "when

hard of hearing children are considered more like than unlike deaf children, the visual channel receives the primary stress in educational management, to the detriment of the auditory channel, which is overwhelmingly more powerful for English language development and educational accomplishments" (Ross 1990, 5).

Even though Ross is referring to hard of hearing children, opponents would argue that hard of hearing children benefit from a stress on their visual orientation. More relevant to the point at hand, however, is the position taken by many mainstream advocates that factors stressing the visual orientation, such as ASL and Deaf culture, are detrimental to educational achievement. Rather, as Ross points out, the auditory orientation that presumably accommodates the norm is superior.

8. Rodda, while believing mainstreaming to be a "desirable" endeavor, also suggests that mainstreaming can adversely affect the positive valuation of the Deaf culture and language (1982). Another study by Harris compares the American Jewish community, whose assimilation into society was made with relative ease, to the African American and Deaf communities, which appear to resist assimilation (1982). For the Jewish community, assimilation came with their choice to accommodate, in contrast to African Americans and Deaf people, for whom "busing" and "mainstreaming" were mandated. Harris suggests that rather than trying to squelch "selective segregation," social scientists should study this phenomenon to determine how it fosters the ultimate goal of assimilation. That mainstreaming remains a controversial issue in the Deaf community is also evident in an article of *Deaf USA*; see Wenokur 1990.

9. For more detailed discussions of the ethnography of communication, see Hymes 1962; Saville-Troike 1989; and Spradley 1979 and 1980.

2

A History of the Deaf Community in America

A study of the Deaf social movement presumes the existence of a community of Deaf people. A number of questions then arise: How did such a community come into being? What factors played a part in its evolution? What is the pattern of life for such a community? What are the ingredients that foster the continued existence of this community? An overview of the historical events chronicling the development of the Deaf community provides context for the issues faced by the Deaf social movement.

Educational institutions have played a central role in the lives of Deaf people. While for most people school is primarily a place to secure an education, for Deaf people, school means much more. For many Deaf people, school is where they meet other Deaf people, often for the first time; at school they develop socialization patterns and friendships that frequently last throughout their lifetimes; there they meet spouses, acquire a language that accommodates their visual orientation, and become a part of a culture that extends beyond the school years.

The educational system, thus, in its early years, offered an opportunity for Deaf people to build a community, and eventually became the mechanism through which the Deaf social movement would thrive. While the beginnings of the education of Deaf people provided a foundation for community building, outside forces to stimulate educational changes in ensuing years provoked resistance from the Deaf community. As these forces sought to defuse the Deaf community, the Deaf social movement came into being. Even as educational reforms were sought or implemented, resistance from the Deaf movement has served to create a bonding and a strengthening of community. As a result, educational institutions have been instrumental in the inception of the Deaf community, as well as providing sustenance to the community in the face of practices that might otherwise serve to divide the community.

The Inception of Community

The Deaf community evolved in the United States in the nineteenth century, when educational institutions for Deaf people were formally established. Prior to the nineteenth century, educational practices for Deaf people in the United States were limited. Some families who could afford the expense sent their Deaf children abroad to countries that provided instruction specifically for Deaf students. Moreover, the only known "congregation" of Deaf people in America existed on Martha's Vineyard. There, however, Deaf people mingled freely with hearing people who, for the most part, also communicated in sign language, so life for Deaf people on the island was an integrated community, rather than a separate community of Deaf people (Groce 1985).

Most Deaf people probably lived in relative isolation prior to the establishment of educational facilities. After all, unlike on Martha's Vineyard, most hearing people did not sign. Laws that prevailed during the early 1800s also suggest that people who did not speak were perceived to be not as competent as their hearing counterparts (Higgins 1988). In New York, for example, Deaf people could not vote. Many states ruled that Deaf people could not be held responsible for criminal acts. Ship owners arriving in the United States were required to report any Deaf people on board and to pay a bond to prevent them from becoming public charges. Several states enacted similar laws to prevent carnivals from bringing Deaf people with them into towns only to abandon them (Best 1943).

Consequently, the United States did not consider the pursuit of education as a worthy endeavor for Deaf people until the nine-teenth century. The first permanent school for the "deaf and dumb" was established in 1817 in Hartford, Connecticut, largely through the efforts of three men. Mason Fitch Cogswell had a Deaf daughter, Alice, who attracted the attention of neighbor Thomas Hopkins Gallaudet. Gallaudet was a minister who appar-ently took interest in Alice as a result of his missionary ventures. Cogswell persuaded Gallaudet to go abroad to study the available educational practices for Deaf students, with the aspiration of establishing a similar endeavor in the United States.

In England, Gallaudet encountered frustration in his dealings with the Braidwoods, the family that dominated the formal edu-cation of Deaf people in the area. The Braidwoods, who practiced oralism (the use of speech and speechreading) in their teachings, viewed their work as a profit-making venture and preferred to keep their craft a family secret. They were willing, however, to apprentice Gallaudet for a number of years, if he would also adopt their tradition of a profit-making institution and not reveal their secrets. This proposal did not appeal to Gallaudet's charitable nature, so when Gallaudet learned that the Abbé Sicard, head of the Royal Institution in Paris, would present an exhibition in London, he made plans to attend.

Gallaudet was impressed with the exhibition, where former Deaf students from the Paris school demonstrated their abilities. One of these former students, Laurent Clerc, was at the time a teacher at the Royal Institution. As a result, Gallaudet moved on to Paris and eventually succeeded in persuading Clerc to return to America with him. Upon their return, Gallaudet, Clerc, and Cogswell founded the school in Hartford as the first permanent American school for the Deaf.

The school became the setting for the emergence of the Ameri-can Deaf community. Shortly afterwards, other schools were es-tablished for Deaf pupils in other states, often by people who were themselves Deaf. American Sign Language (ASL) was also a phenomenon that developed naturally among these Deaf pio-neers. While traveling from France to America on a lengthy ship journey, Clerc had taught Gallaudet a form of signed French (the intent of which was to sign in spoken French word order), and Gallaudet taught Clerc English, and they worked together to create signs that they thought would befit American culture (Lane 1980). Thus, the earliest form of instruction for Deaf students was conducted in what was called "methodical signing," a combination of signed French and signed English (signs in spoken English order).

However, by 1835, educational institutions in America had discarded methodical signing in favor of the sign language that emerged naturally from the Deaf students themselves (Lou 1988). The reason for this change was that Deaf children consistently communicated among themselves in a form of natural signing (later to be called American Sign Language) and educators realized the importance of teaching them by using what came naturally to them. After all, a line from Racine, "To the smallest of the birds, He gives their crumbs" requires forty-eight signs when using methodical French signing (Lane 1984, 62).

So instrumental was this natural form of sign language in binding Deaf people together that Deaf people came to cherish the community that became very much a part of their lives at residential schools. One way to remain within this community was for Deaf people to secure jobs at residential schools upon graduation. Accordingly, by 1851, 36 percent of the teachers were Deaf and this increased to a peak of 42.5 percent in 1870 (J. Jones 1918, 12). Deaf people also began to take the initiative in their own education. Between 1817 and 1911, twenty-four schools for the Deaf were founded by people who were themselves Deaf (Gannon 1981, 19).

However, many Deaf people who could not, or didn't want to, obtain jobs at residential schools still wanted to remain within their community. Consequently, some Deaf people proposed that the Deaf community could and should become a demographic reality. The idea of a Deaf "commonwealth" was first entertained in secrecy by a small group of Deaf people as early as 1831 (Booth 1858). Laurent Clerc also contemplated reserving a portion of land donated by Congress to use as a place for Deaf people to migrate after graduation, although he later explained "a mature deliberation on the whole matter, had made it appear an impracticable plan" (cited in Chamberlain 1858, 212). In 1855, the idea was formally proposed by John J. Flournoy, a Deaf man from the South, whose outlined ideas included purchasing land out in the "West" where Deaf people could assume governing rights (Flournoy 1856). Although Flournoy's proposal became a hotly contested issue, a Deaf commonwealth never materialized. Even so, these proposals for a separate Deaf sphere demonstrate a desire for an extension of a community outside of the school. Further, such proposals were entertained primarily as a result of the integral role of the educational institution in fostering community.

This flourishing Deaf community, however appealing to many Deaf people, was perceived as an antithesis to American society. To many members of the dominant society, the integration of Deaf people into society—rather than their separation from society—was necessary for their success and well-being.

The Educational System Becomes a Battleground

As a result of the perception that Deaf people could be deemed successful only if they entered the mainstream of society, many outside the Deaf community saw the flourishing, yet increasingly separate, community of Deaf people as undesirable. Since the best avenue to curtail the increasing separation of the Deaf community was through the educational system, reformers chose this route. The reformers also sought to eradicate sign language, since it was the binding force of the Deaf community and, they believed, isolated the community from the speaking world. Consequently, the reformists set about to eliminate sign language from the instruction of Deaf people and replace it with speech and speechreading.

Two crucial events marked this shift from sign language to oralism: the second International Congress on Education of the Deaf in Milan in 1880, and the vigorous crusade of Alexander Graham Bell. The Milan Congress, comprised of 163 hearing educators and one Deaf educator from several countries, passed almost unanimously (158 to 6) a resolution that only the oral approach should be used as a medium of instruction for Deaf students. The media, particularly the *London Times,* gave positive coverage to the event, pointing to two indicators of the shift to oralism (Gallaudet 1881). One was the impression that a vast majority of educators from different countries had given their support to the oral approach. Second, an exhibition at the convention had presumably demonstrated the success of oral teaching. Deaf Italian students were able to speak and appeared to be able to speechread and respond accordingly without effort.

However, some of the Milan participants described how the Deaf Italian students had begun answering the questions even before the questioner had finished, which led to speculation that the demonstrations had been rehearsed beforehand (Gallaudet 1881). Further, there was no indication as to how much residual hearing the students possessed. Basically, there was no evidence that these students spoke or speechread as a result of receiving oral instruction. However, the oralists used demonstrations such as those with the Deaf Italian students successfully with the public and the media, who for the most part had little or no expertise with the issues involved in educating Deaf people.

Bell took advantage of this national mood to make his case for Deaf people to use speech. He argued, "It is important for the preservation of our national existence that the people of this country should speak one tongue" (National Education Association 1885, 21). Bell undertook many activities to espouse his views. He wrote numerous articles, put on exhibitions demonstrating the speaking and speechreading abilities of Deaf people, testified on behalf of the oral approach, began publication of the *Volta Review* (a staunchly oralist journal still in existence), and formed the American Association to Promote the Teaching of Speech to the Deaf (the present-day Alexander Graham Bell Association for the Deaf).

The exhibitions Bell put on were reminiscent of the one at the Milan Congress. Bell, a master showman, presented elaborate

Alexander Graham Bell was a staunch advocate of the oral method of educating deaf children.

demonstrations of Deaf people who could speak. In what was probably the case with the Milan exhibition, at one such demonstration, two of his students could hear well and had already acquired the ability to speak prior to becoming his students. Another one of his students on display was actually Deaf, so he had her recite the Lord's Prayer, which he shrewdly calculated would enable the audience to follow her recitation, even if her enunciation was not clear, because the attendees already knew the words (Van Cleve and Crouch 1989).

The results of the Milan Congress, as well as Alexander Graham Bell's crusade, played on the mood of the United States at a time of increasing immigration into the country. According to Leibowitz (1976), a review of the history of education in the United States illustrates that during the mid-1800s, official policy remained impartial in reference to the language of instruction in schools where predominantly non-English speakers were in attendance. Beginning with the 1880s, however, a noticeable shift in official policy was evident in the heavy emphasis on English as the language of instruction in schools. Leibowitz contends this move was due in large part to the crusade to bar new immigrants from educational privileges as well as other citizenship rights.[1] The growing resentment toward immigrants thus became a resentment of difference. Immigrants were "different," as were Deaf people.

Even though these efforts were centered on educational practices for Deaf people, they threatened the demise of the adult Deaf community. Sign language was, after all, the necessary glue that bound them together. As dominant practices used the educational system as a tool to eradicate sign language and, thus, the Deaf community, the Deaf social movement responded by likewise using the education of Deaf people to preserve their cultural identity.

Preserving the Community

So important was sign language to the Deaf community that they were willing to compromise rather than watch educational institutions convert to pure oralism. Compromise was perceived as a necessary step, since oral proponents were swiftly gaining momentum in the United States. Thus, some sign language advocates began pushing for the "combined system" to possibly reduce the polarization between the two camps. The proposed combined system referred to the provision of speech training for those who could benefit from it, in addition to instruction in sign language. The combined system differs from today's widely used "simultaneous communication": where the combined method treats sign language and speech as two separate modalities, simultaneous communication combines the two modalities simultaneously (signing and talking at the same time) (Lou 1988).

The combined system was proposed by Edward Miner Gallaudet. As the son of Thomas Hopkins Gallaudet and his Deaf wife, as well as founder and president of the National Deaf-

Mute College (today's Gallaudet University), the well-respected Edward Miner Gallaudet was in a position to influence Deaf people. Gallaudet was able to sell the notion of the combined system to the Deaf community. The Deaf community then prepared a coalition to reverse the results of the Milan Congress of twenty years earlier. They were ready to offer the compromise of the combined system at the fourth International Congress on the Education and Welfare of the Deaf in Paris in 1900.

At the Milan Congress twenty years earlier, there had been only one Deaf representative. This time around, Deaf people were ready to comprise a large voting bloc. A large Deaf congregation was indeed in attendance at the fourth congress—there were over two hundred Deaf people there, in contrast to over one hundred hearing people (Fay 1900). However, their efforts to build a coalition were thwarted when a decision was reached a year before the conference to hold separate meetings for Deaf and hearing

Edward Miner Gallaudet was the founder and first president of the institution now known as Gallaudet University.

people. At the conference, a proposal was made to combine the two groups. This proposal was ruled out of order by the president, Dr. Ladreit de Lacharriere, a hearing man. His rationale was that the translations between speech and sign would be too confusing and time consuming (Lane 1984).

However, because the Deaf-to-hearing delegate ratio was large, the possibility of reversing the Milan resolutions remained. Consequently, de Lacharriere ruled that Deaf people would not be allowed to even vote. The Congress rejected the resolutions from the Deaf section. In fact, the Congress rebuffed all recommendations to include the Deaf section in any way. As a result, the Congress succeeded in preserving the original Milan resolutions by rejecting the combined system. A further irony at the fourth Congress was that the membership attempted to pass resolutions to create sheltered workshops and organizations to "protect" Deaf people because, for instance, Deaf women could not marry or enter the job market (Lane 1984, 412). As Lane points out, these resolutions to "protect" Deaf people directly contradicted the tenets of oralism that purportedly "restored" Deaf people to society.

Despite the best efforts of the Deaf community, the oralists prevailed for the next sixty or so years. Although the oralists succeeded in banishing sign language, for the most part, from the classroom, the Deaf community persevered through venues such as the National Association of the Deaf and other Deaf-run organizations. During this time the movement continued its efforts to reinstate sign language in the classroom, but for the most part the wellsprings of a Deaf community within the educational system were blocked. The movement turned its attention to other matters. During this time period, the movement sought to preserve the right of Deaf people to drive, battled discriminatory hiring practices, repudiated hearing aid dealers for fraudulent operations, and condemned Deaf "peddlers" for giving the rest of the community a bad name (Gannon 1981). Meanwhile, the increasing lack of access to the educational venue took its toll. The ban on sign language in the classroom paved the way toward decreasing numbers of Deaf people in teaching and decision-making positions. Deaf teachers declined from a peak of 42.5 percent in 1870 (J. Jones, 1918, 12) to 11.7 percent in 1961 (Doctor 1962, 158). Of the meager number of Deaf teachers in the 1960s, most were teachers in manual trades (Lane 1984, 371).

Oralism continued to dominate the education of Deaf people until the late 1960s. By then, a number of factors made it possible for sign language to once again become a viable option in the instruction of Deaf students. Many educators were becoming disenchanted with oralism and its inadequate results (Lou 1988). William C. Stokoe had also published groundbreaking research results that validated American Sign Language as an authentic language (1960). Researchers were also presenting evidence indicating the superior academic achievements of Deaf children of Deaf parents as compared to Deaf children of hearing parents (Brasel and Quigley 1977; Meadow 1967; Stuckless and Birch 1966; Vernon and Koh 1970). Since most Deaf parents used sign language, it was argued that the use of sign language with Deaf children in early childhood was a critical factor contributing to the demonstrated superior academic competence of Deaf children of Deaf parents.

However, it was not American Sign Language itself that was used as a language in classrooms. Rather, most educators adopted "total communication" policies, a descendant of the "combined system." Since total communication is a philosophy that espouses any and all modalities that best fit each individual child's needs, it became a practice to leave the determination of what constituted the best means of communication to each educator. Further, American Sign Language was perceived by many educators as an impoverished language in comparison to the English language. Thus, educators made it a practice to create an abundance of communication methodologies and invented sign systems that adopted the tenets of speech or the English language.

Accordingly, a number of invented sign systems were developed by educators who wanted to present a visual model of English for Deaf children, the rationale being that since ASL did not follow the English grammatical structure, these sign systems were necessary to facilitate the learning of English by Deaf children. Thus, all kinds of sign systems—including Seeing Essential English (SEE), Linguistics of Visual English (LOVE), Signing Exact English (SEE 2), Signed English, just to name a few—were deemed appropriate by educators.

These sign systems were yet another tool to defuse the Deaf community. For Deaf people, these sign systems often created confusion and frustration. The success of retaining these signs depended on memorization of a language that Deaf children often did not even know yet. Further, these inventions were based on phonetic systems. For instance, "butterfly" became "butter" and "fly," which if evaluated for conceptual accuracy in ASL, would mean a piece of butter flying through the air.

These sign systems were also artificial and stilted, as one word could become several signs, for instance, "lovingly" became "love-ing-ly." Even though these systems were unnatural as well as difficult, proponents prevailed by arguing that this was the only way for Deaf people to learn the English language. An additional problem was that because each school adopted whatever system they preferred, the system failed to encourage consistency in sign production or semantics. Researcher Sue Mather warns that such inconsistency can create a "Tower of Deaf Babel" (1990). To illustrate her point, she pointed to the word *diet,* which is normally fingerspelled by Deaf people. She noticed, however, that some teachers used the sign incorrectly—one signed it as "I am on a depression," and another signed it as "I am on a thin round pole" (Mather 1990, 89).

After years of oral domination, the challenges of bringing sign language back into the classroom via total communication—rather than resolving the age-old controversy—have continued to plague the Deaf community. Thus, the Deaf social movement has continued to address issues that center around communication. Educational institutions have provided a mechanism to sustain these controversies and, consequently, to keep the Deaf social movement alive.

The Era of Social Engineering

Even when communication is not explicitly at issue, educational practices and social engineering efforts continue to stimulate the Deaf social movement. A case in point is legislation such as Public Law 94-142, designed to promote mainstreaming for disabled, and by that categorization Deaf, children in public schools. Bell initiated this trend by promoting day schools as a means of drastically reducing socialization opportunities for Deaf students, a critical component of residential schools, and the bonding force of the Deaf community. Within the newer context of Public Law 94-142, advocates of mainstreaming sought to promote integration as a response to growing deinstitutionalizing practices. Since mainstreaming is another practice that is perceived by the Deaf social movement as antagonistic to the interests of Deaf students, Deaf people have rallied to preserve residential schools for the Deaf, as well as to condemn mainstreaming as a feasible option for *all Deaf children.*

Even though educational practices have been at the forefront of battles waged by the dominant society and the Deaf social movement, the Deaf community has also struggled for the right to full participation in the public sphere. The Deaf community strived to achieve civil rights in employment and accommodations in public institutions. Deaf people, in a political move, allied with disabled groups to push through amendments that became Sections 501, 502, 503, and 504 of the Rehabilitation Act of 1973. These laws prohibited discrimination against Deaf and disabled people in institutions receiving a certain amount of federal funding, as well as making provisions for "reasonable accommodation" in these establishments.[2]

This was an era in which Deaf people also fought for their right to sit on juries.[3] For years, and to some extent even today, courts have upheld decisions to exclude Deaf people from juries on the premise that an interpreter would violate the restriction of a twelve-person jury, by constituting the thirteenth person. Another argument for refusing Deaf people jury duty was the use of a different language. Similar acts were undertaken by Deaf people to challenge other civil liberties that barred their full participation in the public sphere.

During this period also, Deaf people sought access to the media. Captions on television came upon the scene only as recently as the 1970s and provided Deaf people with access to a medium previously largely denied to them. With the advent of captions, Deaf people also became more aware of what they had missed. As a result, many Deaf people protested at local stations of a television network that had resisted captioning their programs. Deaf people also became more cognizant of the inaccurate portrayals of Deaf characters in film and television. Consequently, actions were taken at different times to boycott *Voices* and *Calendar Girl,* films that had hearing actors play Deaf characters. This and other endeavors to decry similar practices, although not always taken seriously by Hollywood, have increased the number of Deaf people playing Deaf roles: between 1970 and 1979, 33 percent of these roles were played by Deaf people, while between 1980 and 1986, 75 percent of these roles were played by Deaf people (Schuchman 1988, 96).

These endeavors to participate fully in the public sphere also corresponded to the desire to achieve influence over the educational practices of Deaf students. Educational institutions were, after all, the vehicle through which the Deaf community had gained prominence. Operations throughout history to control the communication practices of Deaf people were achieved through the educational avenue. Accordingly, it should come as no surprise to see the Deaf community carry out its most successful movement—the Gallaudet protest—at the premier educational institution for Deaf people throughout the world.

The Movement toward Deaf Ownership

The Gallaudet movement was significant in its symbolism of the years of struggle between the dominant society and the Deaf community. As an educational institution, Gallaudet served as the archetype for the Deaf community's search for a broader significance—the dispelling of the paternalistic control over Deaf people—by using the educational system as the medium. The previous battles over oralism versus sign language and the various communication systems began primarily because the Deaf community did not have influence over decisions that affected them. The Gallaudet protest over the selection of yet another hearing president is illustrative of the struggle to gain access to decision-making practices.

Although the Gallaudet movement symbolized Deaf ownership for Deaf people, Gallaudet represented much more to Deaf people than merely a center of higher education. Gallaudet's status as the world's only liberal arts college for Deaf students, and its location in the capital of the United States, placed it as a model for other institutions. Further, that a Deaf person could take the helm of a large educational center sent the message that Deaf people across the country could also take over the decision-making process at other schools for the Deaf.

For the Deaf social movement, there are many compelling reasons for Deaf people to play significant roles in the educational process. One crucial reason is that Deaf people, because they have considerable expertise in the Deaf experience, have a unique understanding of the communication needs of the Deaf community. Consequently, Deaf people in positions of leadership at schools or programs for Deaf students will be better able to push for the implementation of sign language instruction at the very least, and bilingual and multicultural instruction at the most.

Accordingly, along with a steady increase in Deaf superintendents[4] and Deaf board members in schools across the United States after the Gallaudet success, a gradual emergence in bilingual and multicultural education has become evident. In the context of education of Deaf people, a bilingual and multicultural program refers to the use of American Sign Language as a medium of instruction. Further, ASL and English are taught as two separate languages—ASL in everyday communication and English as written and/or spoken (for those who can benefit) modalities. Deaf students are also taught to respect the differing cultures of Deaf and hearing people.

To date, bilingual and multicultural programs have been established in various stages of advancement at the California School for the Deaf in Fremont, the Indiana School for the Deaf, the Learning Center for Deaf Children in Massachusetts, the Maryland School for the Deaf, the Metro Deaf School in Minneapolis, the Texas School for the Deaf, and the Wisconsin School for the Deaf. The Kendall Demonstration Elementary School for the Deaf and the Model Secondary School for the Deaf retain their total communication policies, but at the beginning of the 1991–1992 school year, the faculty were "strongly encouraged to sign without voice and to use ASL in the classroom" ("Pre-college Teachers" 1991, 1). So controversial is this approach, however, that even before the year was over, the dominant viewpoint holding that bilingualism is detrimental to the learning process of Deaf children prevailed, and as a result, these schools were directed to adhere to their total communication policy. Currently, other schools continue to explore making changes in their communication policies as well. These recent trends in the instruction of Deaf students espouse a position closer to the heart of the Deaf movement.

Outside the educational system, the implications of the Gallaudet movement have created a more vocal demand for full participation in the public sphere as well. Local efforts in a number of states to protest inadequate 911 responses to Deaf callers that resulted in deaths (e.g., Munoz 1991), rallies to implement relay systems to enable Deaf and hearing callers to communicate over the telephone, coalition efforts with disabled groups to pass the Americans with Disabilities Act (ADA),[5] which bans discrimination on a wider scale than previous legislation, as well as more recent efforts to promote placement for Deaf children on the basis of individual needs versus that of "full inclusion," and mandated captioning on all videotapes, comprise much of the action after the protest.

Even so, the Deaf social movement continues to flourish because Deaf people still do not have full access to public life. A poll of the Deaf community by *Deaf Life* in 1988 demonstrates that an overwhelming majority—98 percent—do not believe that Deaf people have yet achieved equal rights in the United States ("Readers' Viewpoint" 1988, 31). One respondent acknowledged that Gallaudet was a "huge jump in the right direction," but that hearing people needed "desperately to be educated about the Deaf community by the Deaf community, so that barriers of prejudice & discrimination can be knocked down & the doors of opportunity can be opened" to the Deaf community ("Readers' Viewpoint" 1988, 31). In 1994, the situation had not improved, as indicated in a *Deaf Life* poll that asks if Deaf people have experienced discrimination by virtue of their being Deaf. Out of 321 responses, a resounding 100 percent said yes ("Readers' Responses" 1994, 28).

The American Deaf community, thus, continues to move toward the goal of full participation in public life. However, because the pervasiveness of the struggle between members of the dominant society and the Deaf community over the most appropriate educational practices for Deaf people has so placed the Deaf social movement within the center of the educational system, the movement has for the most part focused on this struggle. Although the Deaf social movement has attended to other issues relating to Deaf civil rights, no other struggle has been so instrumental in fostering a community of Deaf people and of sustaining their movement over the years. This book examines the ideological war created within the educational system, along with its broader societal implications, that has permeated the Deaf community for more than a century.

Notes

1. Leibowitz illustrates this practice on Native Americans. This period marked the establishment of boarding schools for Native American students

located at a distance from reservations (1976). As Leibowitz points out, this practice was designed to "separate the Indian child from his reservation and family, strip him of his tribal lore and mores . . . and prepare him in such a way that he would never return to his people" (452). This practice was made possible due to the emphasis on English as a language of instruction: "English-language instruction and abandonment of the native language became complementary means to the end" (452).

2. See Section 504 (1981) for further information.

3. See Mentkowski (1985) for further information.

4. In the five to six years preceding the Gallaudet protest, there were only four Deaf and hard of hearing school superintendents (Gannon, personal communication, December 5, 1991). In contrast, as of December 1995, there were twenty-two Deaf and hard of hearing superintendents (National Information Center on Deafness Fact Sheet, December 7, 1995).

5. See McCrone (1991) for more information.

3
The Struggle Begins

The contemporary social movement of Deaf people in America has its roots in the historical struggles between the dominant society and Deaf people. So pervasive are the ideological struggles between the dominant culture and the Deaf community that the issues that marked the early Deaf movement remain the basis for today's movement. The early years of the Deaf social movement highlight the ideological contrasts between the dominant society's characterization of Deaf people and their redefinition of themselves.

A focus on the early years reveals the construction of a stigma of *difference* that characterizes the ideological struggle between the dominant culture and the Deaf community. Although from outward appearances Deaf people are no different from anyone else, to be Deaf in most instances requires a different mode of communication—a rather obvious difference. It is to this difference that society reacts. After all, most people use speech to communicate. As such, the dominant society has created an ideology of normality that posits speaking and hearing as *normal*. To maintain the norm, society has resorted to *dividing practices* designed to place Deaf people either out of sight or within the mainstream of society. By isolating Deaf people from society, the "universality" of speaking and hearing is maintained. Even "mainstreaming," which presupposes the acceptance of Deaf people into society, is a dividing practice because it discourages Deaf people from communicating in their most comfortable mode, and thus the norm of speaking and hearing is again revered.

Although dividing practices are intended to reduce the signifying features of Deaf people in order to maintain the norm, they have the opposite effect. Deaf people react by resisting efforts to alter or eradicate their sign language. In fact, the more dividing practices attempt to eliminate sign language, the more strongly Deaf people resist. Thus, sign language binds Deaf people together and ultimately serves to sustain a community of, by, and for Deaf people.

The Roots of Community: Responding to the Ideology of Normality

The central role of sign language in the Deaf community came about in response to the dominant society's strategic isolation of Deaf people from the mainstream. This early stage of the Deaf social movement, which began in the 1820s after the first school for the Deaf in Hartford, Connecticut, was established, can be referred to as the "period of inception" (Griffin 1952, 186). The period of inception is usually the stage that sets the movement in motion. Rather than being an organized collective striving to make social changes that characterize a social movement, this early stage of the Deaf social movement represented a building of community as a symbolic response to the dividing practices of the dominant society. This building of community by Deaf people not only turned their rejection by society into a positive force that empowered Deaf people, but also enabled them to set up the foundation for a social movement. This need for community and for what would become a social movement was inadvertently encouraged by the dominant society's enactment of the ideology of normality.

The tensions between the dominant and dominated are illustrated by the rhetorical processes that the dominant society has developed to define normality and to maintain the definition. Deaf people, in turn, created strategies that responded to the ideology of normality and enabled the establishment of community.

Strategy as used here does not indicate the "conscious" intentionality of either the dominant society or the Deaf social movement to conspire against the other group. Rather, *strategy* is used to refer to the natural phenomenon that emerges as the dominant society and the Deaf social movement struggle constantly to control and to resist.

The Dominant Ideology of Normality

Social movements usually begin as a response to dominant strategies of oppression. Leland Griffin, a rhetorical scholar explains: "Movements begin when some pivotal individual or group—suffering attitudes of alienation in a given social system, and drawn (consciously or unconsciously) by the impious dream of a mythic Order—enacts, gives voice to, a No" (Griffin 1966, 462). An examination of the Deaf social movement and the emergence of their rhetorical "No" necessitates a study of the origins of the movement in the late nineteenth century. The central rhetorical practice through which the dominant society contextualizes Deaf people is the strategy of normality. Normality is a set of practices that surround a material characteristic with the common attributes of the dominant society. The concept of normality carries comfort for many people because it validates the familiar. The unfamiliar generates fear because it stresses the unknown. People thus revere normality because it does not require them to change their daily habits. Normality becomes an important feature to be maintained. Accordingly, the dominant society develops rhetorical mechanisms to sustain the familiar by controlling the power to define normality.

Dominant groups who sustain normality also maintain their social position. Foucault's explanation of the rhetorical construct of normality is useful in demonstrating how this process creates "abnormality" and, consequently, sustains the power of the dominant. This process begins in early childhood, with strategies such as "name-calling," when children call each other names based on "peculiarities" in physical traits, names, or social relationships (Farb 1974). This tactic very effectively "arouse[s] our contempt so that we'll dismiss" the intended victims (Woolfolk Cross 1989, 91). To define others is to maintain control over them and to preserve the status quo. As Haig Bosmajian, who writes about language and oppression, points out, the word *define* comes from the Latin word *definire*, which means "to limit" (Bosmajian 1983, 5). Bosmajian goes on to say, "Through definition, we restrict, we set boundaries, we name" (5). The strategy of normality is then carried further to become a rhetorical basis for the social practice of treatment. The rhetoric of normality gives rise to languages of condemnation and correction.

The rhetorical constructs of "normality" and "abnormality" are strategies to establish a hierarchy that places the "normal" in the superior position. The ideology of "normality" is actually an abstraction created by the dominant society. Foucault (1970) explains that "normality" is a rhetorical construct created to legitimize its definition and to further maintain control over a group by rhetorical enforcement. As such, society elevates common characteristics shared by large numbers of people and thus constitutes and legitimizes the establishment of a norm. The norm is then used to define the "normal." What was previously arbitrary becomes a defining characteristic. A categorization of normality likewise defines those who do not fit into the category, those who do not conform—as "abnormal."

The ideology of normality is so pervasive that enforcing it in a society is no more difficult than labeling any deviation from the norm a "defect." Such a defect is termed a stigma by the sociologist Erving Goffman, in that the stigmatized person is "reduced in our minds from a whole and usual person to a tainted, discounted one" (Goffman 1963, 3). Commonalities are thus sanctioned and differences condemned. As such, normality is a strategy to maintain the status quo and in turn generates a language of domination.

A society's strategy of normality easily moves from domination to languages of condemnation and correction. Foucault notes, in tracing the discourse of deviance, that historically dominant societies have to "punish" the "deviant," and agents of the human sciences in these societies have committed themselves to "correct" the "defect" (1977). Indeed, the strategy of "defining" the "deviant" to maintain control over them goes back a long way. Andrew King, a rhetorical scholar, wrote that God gave Adam and Eve power over the planet by giving them the right to name the creatures of Eden, and that Socrates controlled others when they accepted his definitions (1987). Bosmajian illustrates how the persecution of Jewish people in Nazi Germany, which began with definitive labels such as "disease(s)," "parasites," "Jewish bacilli," and labels of Native Americans by the newcomers as "savages," and "uncivilized," led to the justification of cruel and inhumane treatment toward them (1983; 1992).

As the nineteenth century came to terms with difference, the strategy of normality spread through rhetorical practices to the domination, condemnation, and correction of Deaf people. One such practice was to label Deaf people "mentally deficient." This perception of Deaf people as "mentally deficient," or more commonly "dumb," stems from as far back as 355 B.C. when Aristotle said of Deaf people: "Men that are deaf are in all cases also dumb; that is, they can make vocal sounds, but they cannot speak" (Aristotle 1910, 7). In the earlier days, the Greek word for "dumb" also meant "speechless" and did not necessarily refer to one's mental ability (Bender 1970). However, for many years afterward, Aristotle's statement was taken to mean literally that Deaf people were "dumb." Interpretations in later years included statements such as: "Those who are born deaf all become senseless and incapable of reason" (Hodgson 1954, 62). By the eighteenth century, the Enlightenment's elevation of mental reasoning transformed "dumb" into "subhuman." In the words of a Swiss doctor, "What stupidity we find in most of these unfortunate deaf! How little they differ from animals!" (Amman 1873, 2). By labeling Deaf people as a lesser species, the dominant society constituted Deaf people as beings that could not adequately care for themselves, thus authorizing society to undertake that responsibility.

It then became society's task to devise ways of improving the status of Deaf people as human beings. Rhetorically, this manifested itself as efforts to correct the "defect."

The strategy of definition and dehumanization paved the way for the practice of correction. At the very extreme, this rhetoric authorized actual experimentation on Deaf people to "correct" their sense of hearing. For example, Prosper Ménière, a physician at a residential school for the Deaf in France, reported that his predecessor, Jean-Marc Itard, thought nothing of performing numerous experiments on Deaf students, including applying electricity into their ears, placing leeches on their necks, and other such monstrosities, which often resulted in serious infections, not to mention several accidents and deaths. Although Ménière himself did not condone such torturous practices, he justified the need for correction: "The deaf believe that they are our equals in all respects. We should be generous and not destroy that illusion. But whatever they believe, deafness is an infirmity and we should repair it whether the person who has it is disturbed by it or not" (Lane 1984, 134). In the logic of correction, the best way to "correct" the "defect" was for Deaf people to gain the sense of hearing. If Deaf people could hear, then they would be "normal" like the dominant culture.

Accompanying strategies to correct the sense of hearing were methods to teach Deaf people to speak. The ability to use the dominant mode of communication would normalize Deaf people. As a biographer of Jacob Rodrigo Pereira, one of the foremost advocates of teaching speech to Deaf people, promised in a tribute to Pereira in 1939: "There will be no more deaf-mutes. There will be deaf speaking ones" (Bender 1970, 77). Consider oralist educator Carroll G. Pearse's narrative of the teaching method:

> The teacher utters a sound or a word; the child is led to try to imitate, and use his own organs of speech. He has difficulty; the teacher illustrates again, and again he tries. . . . He is shown in utmost detail and with infinite repetition how every organ of speech must act to produce the sounds which make up spoken language. . . . His voice, at first unnatural and artificial as though squeaked out by a machine, becomes

more and more nearly natural, and by the time he passes the grades of the elementary school he shows very little, by his voice, that he cannot hear. (Pearse 1912, 1–2)

The tacit background of Pearse's description is the child's natural desire to speak. The method is built on the imitation of the superior teacher's normal speech. Pearse describes an exacting effort to "correct" the "defect." Rhetorically, the goal is established: Not until Deaf people transform their "unnatural and artificial" speech into the "nearly natural" can a Deaf person almost pass for normal.

The elevation of speech as the normal mode of communication—"the only way of restoring the deaf-mute to society" was to "give him the power of conversing like hearing persons"—denigrated sign language as abnormal (cited in Hartman 1881, 125). The attack on sign language was overt, it was demeaned as "violent and spasmodic miming, [in] which [Deaf people] can at best simply establish their kinship with the famous primates" (cited in Lane 1984, 409). Pearse, who had described his teaching of speech so carefully, labeled Deaf people who used sign language as "freaks" and "dummies," comparable to dogs who were trained to perform only for their masters (Pearse 1912, 2).

Creating Community by Undermining the Ideology of Normality

By constructing abnormality, the dominant society was able to transform rhetoric into the institutional and structural oppression of Deaf people. In the words of a Deaf man who proposed the establishment of a separate Deaf state, Deaf people were "contemned [sic] spurned, degraded and abhorred" by hearing people (Flournoy 1856, 124). This rhetorical condemnation of Deaf people in early America made it possible to shun Deaf people from the mainstream of society. Such practices were common in the early part of the century, when people with mental retardation, mental illnesses, leprosy, and cerebral palsy were considered a "menace" to society and, therefore, placed out of sight in segregated institutions (Shapiro 1994). In keeping with national trends to separate the "abnormal" from the "normal," dividing practices segregated Deaf people together in residential schools, or what at the time were called "asylums." By keeping "abnormal" people out of sight and, in turn, out of mind, society could live in a world of "normal" people.

By segregating Deaf people from society, the dominant culture inadvertently gave rise to a form of separatism that Deaf people turned to their advantage. Since Deaf people were not welcome in the public sphere, they created a Deaf community, or what they at the time called "a class" or "common community" of Deaf people (e.g., Flournoy 1856; Rider 1877). The evolution of a separate sphere for Deaf people enabled them to build a community on their own terms.

The response of the Deaf community to the charge of "abnormality" demonstrates how social movements can turn the symbol of their oppression into a symbol of unity. Sign language became the distinction that gave dignity to the Deaf community and transformed the "abnormal" into the "distinguished" by creating a reversal of the hierarchy. The reversal of hierarchy, in turn, established the stature of their distinction and enabled the community to create its own institutions. This structural development provided the community with space in which to create their own discourse and to define normality on their own terms.

Since the modality of speech was constituted by society as a necessity for normality, Deaf people were for the most part excluded. And since Deaf people were frequently defined as subhuman, society had determined that Deaf people were not capable of thought or using language to convey thought. However, the development of a language of signs made it possible for Deaf people to prove that society was mistaken in their views. Sign language made it possible for Deaf people to communicate. Sign language made it possible for Deaf people to express their thoughts. Indeed, it was sign language that made Deaf people "normal."

Even though sign language did not fit into the universal definition of normality, the shunning of Deaf people from society made it possible for Deaf people to create their own definition of normality. And in this definition, sign language played a key role. The strategy of sign language was to turn their difference into an integral part of their community. In this way sign language served to bind Deaf people together as a "class." Further, sign language defied the dominant position that placed speech as the domain of "proper" communication. John J. Flournoy, a Deaf man who advocated the formation of a separate community for Deaf people, aptly expresses this sentiment: "We are not beasts, for all our deafness! We are MEN! The Era of de l'Épée has been the epocha [sic] of our birth of mind. After a long night of wandering, our planet has at length attained an orbit around a central luminary" (Flournoy 1858, 149–50). The significance of sign language was that it enabled Deaf people to declare themselves to be more than beasts. By declaring themselves to be people, Deaf people could place themselves on a plane equal to the rest of society. However, sign language would continue to be the feature that distinguished Deaf people from hearing people. The "central luminary" represented sign language. And since sign language was central only in the Deaf community, Flournoy could only arrive "home" in this community. As such, Flournoy's "central luminary" symbolized sign language as the salvation of Deaf people, as well as the centrality of sign language as the bonding factor of the Deaf community.

The role of sign language as a binding factor of the Deaf community has been especially significant, considering that most Deaf people are born to hearing families. Approximately 90–95 percent of Deaf children are born to hearing parents (Best 1943; Rainer and Deming 1963; Schein and Delk 1974); in fact, that figure may be higher, in that "only about 4 percent . . . have two deaf parents; an even smaller percentage have one hearing impaired and one normally hearing parent" (Jordan and Karchmer 1986, 137). To compound the issue, many Deaf children did not and still do not share the communication mode used by their families.

And if, during that era, Deaf children were not provided with opportunities to develop and express their thoughts, it would be extremely likely that they shared Flournoy's sense of feeling lost; that is, until they were introduced to such an opportunity. As Flournoy declared, sign language provided such an avenue.

Since Deaf people were segregated together in residential schools and even encouraged to use sign language, it very quickly became a cherished part of their daily lives. Further, because sign language was a modality shared primarily with other Deaf people and not the dominant society, this difference naturally drew Deaf people closer together. And this difference fostered the growth of a self-governed Deaf community. Since society did not value sign language as a communication commodity the way Deaf people did, it would also be necessary for Deaf people to create a hierarchy that would give the highest order to sign language. Accordingly, social organizations founded by Deaf people, such as the New England Gallaudet Association of Deaf-Mutes, celebrated this hierarchy.

The language of their constitution employed the term "mute" throughout, including a reference to "our mute community," an allusion to Deaf people who did not speak (Chamberlain 1857, 79). Under the terms of requirements for membership, the first section determined that "mute" people could join. The second section added that "only deaf" people or those who "have never been in any institution for deaf-mutes," in reference to speaking Deaf people, could also become members (81). It was not until later that hearing people were mentioned. They were, however, not invited to join; instead, their status was relegated to an invitation to subscribe to their periodicals.

That there was a need to distinguish among "mutes," "only deaf" people, and hearing people is significant. These differences centered primarily around the use of sign language. Deaf people who used sign language demonstrated a stronger Deaf identity than those who did not. Although "only deaf" people were allowed to join the social organizations, Deaf people still felt the need to establish separate categories of "mute" and "only deaf" people. This illustrates the perception of the difference between the two groups of Deaf people. Further, the order in which the categorizations appeared is enlightening. The position of "mutes" in the constitution gave rise to the establishment of a hierarchy that gave the highest rank to signing Deaf people. As such, Deaf people who spoke were placed in the middle, and hearing people at the bottom of the hierarchy. This hierarchy exalted in the Deaf community was in direct contrast to the dominant social order.

At the fourth International Congress on Education of the Deaf in 1900, the hierarchy created by Deaf people was further strengthened in the rhetoric of a Deaf leader. James L. Smith, the sixth president of the National Association of the Deaf, an advocacy organization established by Deaf people, addressed the Deaf section, which had been excluded from participation in all decisions that would affect them:

> Government derives its power from the consent of the governed— but not when it comes to the affairs of the deaf. . . . We protest in vain. Our petitions addressed to governments receive no response, our resolutions at national and international congresses are ignored. . . . In fact, the deaf are in a better position to judge these issues than the hearing. They know what it is to be deaf, they know what it is to have only a single method available for education, they know what it is to be forever blocked in their legitimate demands. (cited in Lane 1984, 413)

The statement that the dominant society did not listen to Deaf people was an assertion that Deaf people lacked power within the dominant hierarchy. Smith further pointed out that hearing people could not adequately represent the concerns of the Deaf community because they had never experienced being Deaf. Smith went on to say that only Deaf people could determine what their best interests were. By declaring that Deaf people had more experience in being Deaf than did hearing people, Smith placed Deaf people in a position superior to hearing people. In so doing, he reversed the structural hierarchy, thus granting power to Deaf people.

However, a reversal of the hierarchy could not function in the dominant society. It was then necessary for Deaf people to create their own world, separate from that of the dominant society. In this new world, Deaf people would be in control of their destinies. Smith enticed his audience with this possibility, by calling for "all present to join together to affirm a new declaration of human rights, the right of the deaf to life, liberty, the pursuit of happiness, and the education of their children on a plan they accept" (Lane 1984, 413). The call for the creation of a new social order was accompanied by doubts that Deaf people would ever achieve the democratic ideals espoused in the Declaration of Independence. Only by creating their own declaration, on their own terms, could they achieve true equality. The dominant society's efforts to prevent Deaf people from determining what was in their own best interests helped sustain and foster the concept of a Deaf community. The marginalization of Deaf people by the dominant society thus constituted a form of "separatism."

As such, sign language and the reversal of a Deaf hierarchy legitimized formal institutions such as the Deaf marriage and "family," organizations established for Deaf people, and publications that furthered the growing network of Deaf people. Prior to the advent of residential schools, Deaf people had little opportunity to meet and marry other Deaf people. However, the congregation of Deaf people in schools fostered an environment in which sign language became so integral to the Deaf community that it was further sustained by the institution of intermarriages. A reversal of the hierarchy placed the utmost importance on sign language. Marriages between Deaf people maintained the hierarchy by affirming the importance of marital unions as places of discourse. A study of marriage patterns among Deaf people gives support to the bonding role of sign language in keeping Deaf marriages intact.

Edward Allen Fay, an educator and author, found that out of a total of 4,471 couples, an astounding 95 percent of Deaf people married other Deaf people (1896). Further, mixed couple marriages (Deaf and hearing) were three times as likely to end in divorce as were Deaf marriages. Since marriages between Deaf people were likely sites for the maintenance of sign language, it is highly likely that Deaf marriages received greater support within the Deaf community than did mixed marriages. In turn, Deaf marriages strengthened the Deaf community by giving credence to sign language and to the community itself.

Deaf people also continued to build community in their establishment of social organizations, which began with the New England Gallaudet Association of Deaf-Mutes in 1854. This initiated a trend toward the formation of social organizations and clubs at primarily local levels, organized and run by Deaf people. Henry Rider, a president of a local organization, noted the importance of these institutions as places for discourse: "To us, [social organizations are] what the oases of the Great Desert are to famishing travelers" (Rider 1877, 251). Indeed, sign language had so deeply drawn Deaf people together that they were constantly seeking ways to create more opportunities to bond together.

Deaf people so cherished their community that they wanted to establish a formal network in which they could not only maintain contact with each other, but also expand their circle of Deaf acquaintances. Accordingly, the notion of publications operated and disseminated by Deaf people became a significant instrument for the maintenance of Deaf discourse.[1] Such publications were either run by independent Deaf owners or organizations or were sponsored by residential schools. The residential school periodicals became so popular that they were fondly dubbed "The Little Paper Family."

Publications were an important strategy for strengthening the community. Since Deaf people were scattered geographically, the publications ensured that Deaf people were kept informed of events and news in the Deaf community. By keeping people informed of social events, the Deaf community could increase the chances of larger attendances at these events. Spreading the news of happenings to other Deaf people also ensured that they kept in touch. The papers routinely listed who had gotten new jobs, and these announcements encouraged Deaf people to branch out into new areas of employment. These publications were a way for Deaf people to take pride in their community, to expand their social and networking horizons, and most important, to maintain their ties to each other.

Strengthening Community by Responding to Attack

The first stage of the Deaf social movement belonged primarily to the "period of inception," which is the stage that usually serves as a prelude to a movement (Griffin 1952, 186). Deaf people responded to their condemnation and rejection by heralding sign language and turning their difference into a symbol of their unity. Their strategic building of the deaf community as a place of discourse was allowed to nurture in relative isolation until their endeavors began to interfere with normalization.

The dominant society reacted to the unity of the Deaf community by shifting rhetorical strategies in order to maintain control over Deaf people. In turn, the Deaf community was compelled to create new strategies to accommodate the change in dominance.

The Attack on the Deaf Community

The placement of Deaf people in residential schools as a means of isolating them from society backfired when this approach paved the way for the self-determination of Deaf people. The segregation of Deaf people had not simply kept them out of sight but had actually enabled them to create their own community in which sign language and institutional foundations were turned into positive achievements.

Dominant discourses then switched gears to strategies of integrating Deaf people under the guise of normalization. This movement paralleled the shift in policies dictating languages of instruction in schools in the United States beginning in the 1880s (Leibowitz 1976). Prior to the 1880s, official policies on languages of instruction in schools were neutral, and many schools taught classes in languages other than English to accommodate immigrants. This tolerance for diversity appeared to change in the 1880s, however, and policies began to require schooling in the majority language—English—and to foster behavioral norms that conformed to that of the majority. A case in point was the establishment of boarding schools for Native American children, away from their reservations and their families, to teach them English and majority customs (Leibowitz 1976). This shift exemplified the perception of integration as a symbol of American democracy by many members of the dominant society. Inherent in the argument for integration is the masking of differences. The argument that the dominant society is "color blind" or does not attend to any other differences lends credibility to the tenets of the American motto, "one nation under God." As such, the convictions of the "democratic" prototype are presented as strictly honorable goals. Under these auspices, the rhetoric of integration is introduced as a respectable endeavor that befits American democratic ideals.

In this vein, the process by which society presents integration as a symbol of American democracy for Deaf people becomes a strategy of normality. The definition of normality carries over to integration. By declaring integration as a normal endeavor of American society, the dominant culture constitutes integration as a legitimate goal for everyone. And if integration is normal, then segregation is abnormal.

Inherent in the strategy of normalization is the desire to control Deaf people. One predominant approach has been to control the communication of Deaf people under the pretext of integrating Deaf people into society. The second International Congress of the Deaf that convened in 1880 serves as a case in point. The Congress in Milan determined that speech alone would be the mode of communication Deaf people would use. The following resolutions were passed:

1. The Convention, considering the incontestable superiority of speech over signs, (1) for restoring deaf-mutes to social life, (2) for giving them greater facility of language, declares that the method of articulation should have preference over that of signs in the instruction and education of the deaf and dumb.

2. Considering that the simultaneous use of signs and speech has the disadvantage of injuring speech and lipreading and precision of ideas, the Convention declares that the pure oral method ought to be preferred. (Gallaudet 1881, 5–6)

Through resolutions such as these at the Milan Congress and other discourse practices that maintain the superiority of speech over sign language, the dominant culture also reaffirms its supremacy. In fact, the prevailing theme of the Milan Congress was that Deaf people could not be considered normal unless they adopted the language and culture of the dominant society. As a participant at the Congress declared, speech was the "Queen" who "tolerates no rivals . . . she renounces all" (cited in Lane 1984, 393). The closing shout from the podium at the Congress was "Vive la parole!" which translates as "Long live speech!" (Lane 1984, 394). These statements marginalize sign language and herald speech, which thereby enables the dominant society to maintain the power structure and preserve their interests.

By positing speech as the necessary attribute with which to enter the public sphere, the dominant culture ensures the inferior status of Deaf people. To ensure that Deaf people do not disrupt the status quo, it is necessary for the dominant society to govern the lives of Deaf people. Thus, participants at the Milan Congress were able to grant themselves permission to control Deaf people by declaring themselves the caretakers of the education of Deaf students. The rhetorical strategies that enable the dominant society to constitute their power while marginalizing Deaf people also give license to the dominant culture to define terms of "access" to "their" society.

The Milan resolutions also illuminated "dividing practices" by employing the rhetoric of method. The Congress stipulated that "the *method* [emphasis added] of articulation should have preference over that of signs in the instruction and education of the deaf and dumb." The language of "method" is a strategy that gives rise to competition by presenting communication as a series of choices. In doing so, the dominant society imposes "dividing practices" by pitting speech against sign language. Since speech has been defined as a normal trait in contrast to sign language, the superiority of speech as a method is validated. Further, by positioning speech as the "method," educators are given the authority to enforce it in the classroom. Speech as method then becomes a tool for education and, therefore, integration. The establishment of "communication as method" became so widespread that it evolved into the "war of methods" that remains today and has served to divide not only Deaf people from hearing people, but Deaf people from Deaf people.[2]

The Milan Congress also gave authority to dominant discourses by documenting resolutions to abolish sign language. By doing so, the Milan Congress paved the way for oralism in America. The resolutions passed there gave legitimacy to oralist advocates like Alexander Graham Bell and to the oral schools already established in the United States as "experiments." By giving rise to dominant discourses that conferred status on speech and other characteristics representing the dominant culture, sign language and other nondominant features were effectively pathologized.

Although the resolutions of the Milan Congress stipulated the goal of oralism as that of integrating Deaf people into society, the wider American society remained for the most part ignorant of the existence of a community of Deaf people. Advocates for integration within the Deaf educational system, such as Alexander Graham Bell, made it their mission to alert the American people to what they perceived to be a growing trend toward separatism. Shortly after the Milan Congress, Bell described the Deaf community as a situation of "great calamity to the world" (Bell 1883, 41). He claimed that society was condoning the spread of "a defective race of human beings" by allowing Deaf people to socialize primarily with each other, establish their own organizations, publish their own newspapers, and marry each other, which, he said, leads to the birth of more Deaf children (Bell 1883, 41). In doing so, he introduced a "threat" that must be treated as a "crisis" by the social order.

This "predicament" was, however, "treatable." Bell proposed implementing "preventive measures," including the establishment of smaller schools and day schools, ideally, with one Deaf child in each school; and co-education with hearing children, which he acknowledged might be impracticable, suggesting, instead, partial co-education and instruction in articulation and speechreading. The ultimate goal should be "integration" of Deaf people to allow the "retention of the normal environment during the period of education" (Bell 1883, 46). To achieve these ends, it would also be necessary to eliminate Deaf teachers, who produce "an environment that is unfavorable to the cultivation of articulation and speech-reading" (Bell 1883, 48).

Bell presented the problem of Deaf separatism as inimical to the interests of society. Through the rhetoric of integration, Bell quite overtly spoke for the destruction of the power structure growing within the Deaf community and a return of the power to the patriarchal society. In this vein, Alexander Graham Bell's arguments corresponded to the "one nation under God" theme of the United States. Not only did residential schools for the Deaf begin to adopt the oral approach in lieu of sign language, but by the 1920s, more and more day schools and classes had been established, paving the way toward an "integration" of Deaf people into society. In 1882, only 7.5 percent of the schools were oral only; by 1919, 80 percent were (Van Cleve and Crouch 1989). In addition, the number of Deaf teachers also decreased from a peak of 42.5 percent in 1870 to 14.5 percent in 1917 (Moores 1978).

Strengthening Community by Direct Response

Deaf people were becoming increasingly concerned about the efforts of Alexander Graham Bell and his associates to fuel the growth of oralism. Deaf people had come to cherish their way of life and were not about to stand by while the movement to eradicate sign language spread. Sign language represented their very being, and most important, it was their salvation on the road toward self-determination. Accordingly, Deaf people developed strategies to preserve their sign language and thwart the efforts of oralist advocates. They sought to strengthen their community by adopting rhetorical strategies to symbolize self-governance and, based on these strategies, to establish a political organization as a site for discourse and networking.

One of the first responses to the attack by the dominant society, that marks the beginning of the Deaf social movement in the United States, was to build up a site specifically for political discourse. The first National Convention of Deaf-Mutes, at which the National Association of Deaf-Mutes (NAD) was formed in 1880, convened to collaborate on "interests peculiar to ourselves which can be taken care of by ourselves" (cited in Gannon 1981, 62; Schein 1989, 74). Although Deaf people had established a community in which sign language symbolized their unity, they needed a setting for political discourse to ward off the threat to their community. The NAD thus provided such a space. In addition, the NAD gave legitimacy to the movement because of its institutional status. The capability of Deaf people to create a political institution demonstrated their competence in self-governance, as well as a force with which the dominant society would have to contend.

To demonstrate their power as a political entity, the NAD adopted several rhetorical strategies. One such strategy was to foster their distinction by celebrating their "muteness." Even though the spread of oralism had prompted many educators to pursue the removal of the term *mute* from institutions because it served as a contradiction to the goal of oralism, the NAD did not drop the term from their organization until their third convention in 1889 (Gannon 1981).

In view of the imposition of speech on their community, it was likely that Deaf people cherished the term because it symbolized the unique status of sign language in their community. Perusals of earlier films show that most Deaf people kept their lips closed while signing, not moving them at all. Thus, the significance of retaining the term *mute* in their organizational name was a political strategy to exemplify the defiance of oralism.

The NAD also adopted the tradition of the rhetorical strategy evident in the emphasis on the "of, by, and for" or simply "of," that was begun by the New England Gallaudet Association. To use "for" in the organizational name denotes the "helping" mind-set. The emphasis on the use of "of, by, and for" was also a political statement that signified their competence in self-governance. The rhetorical intent was carried over into practice. So pervasive was the statement as a symbol of Deaf empowerment that hearing people were excluded from membership in the organization until 1964.

Strengthening Community through Symbolic Reinforcement

Not only did Deaf people respond to the attack on their community by creating rhetorical strategies in a political context, they also endeavored to strengthen their community by enacting symbols that represented their oppression as well as sign language as their salvation.

The rhetoric of crucifixion came to represent confinement as a symbol of oppression for Deaf people. Second, the significance of sign language as the salvation of Deaf people as they took action to preserve it in case the advent of oralism either eradicated sign language, or drastically altered it into an unrecognizable form will be discussed.

The theme of "crucifixion" was a direct response to the desire of the dominant structure to dominate the Deaf "body" by "fixing" it. As Foucault points out, the body is the object of a "political field" (Foucault 1977, 25). He explains that "power relations have an immediate hold upon it [the body]; they invest it, mark it, train it, torture it, force it to carry out tasks, to perform ceremonies, to emit signs" (25). And the ultimate goal is not the transformation of the body, rather it is "increased domination" (138). Accordingly, the rhetoric of crucifixion was a strategy by Deaf people to create a powerful symbol of their oppression.

During an era in which religion played one of the most significant, if not the most pivotal, roles in American lifestyles, the

Christian symbol exuded a powerful appeal.[3] Consequently, the metaphor of crucifixion was adopted in response to events at the fourth Congress, where Deaf and hearing people were separated into two sections and no space was given for Deaf input on their own fate. James L. Smith addressed the Deaf section: "Let us declare to the entire world that the deaf will not be crucified on the cross of a single method" (cited in Lane 1984, 413). This statement captures several important sentiments held by Deaf people. Smith's assertion suggests themes of persecution, confinement, and salvation.

The persecution theme is illustrated in the biblical references, which subliminally create a visual image of Deaf people hung up on a cross. This feeling of persecution is overtly described by Albert Ballin, a Deaf man: "I resented having my lessons hurled at me. It seemed as if all the words, for which I never cared a tinker's damn, were invented for the sole purpose of harassing and tormenting me. . . . How I hated my teacher, my school, the whole creation" (Ballin 1930, 2). Implicitly or explicitly, the theme of persecution symbolized Deaf people suffering for the sins of hearing oppressors who tortured Deaf people by imposing on them the oral modality and taking away their salvation—sign language.

The crucifixion motif reinforces the confinement theme in that it represented the powerlessness of the hands. Deaf people cherish their hands because their hands provide them with their primary means of communication. At the heart of the confinement theme, then, was sign language. The binding of hands for Deaf people was therefore the equivalent of taping the mouths of hearing people. Indeed, Deaf people considered the confinement of their hands a criminal act, and J. Schuyler Long went on to compare the act to that of the binding of babies' feet by Chinese women, and babies' heads by the Flathead Indians (Gallaudet and Hall 1909).

The theme of confinement portrayed the Deaf person as the victim. Powerful images such as these were strategies to portray as an illusion the self-created role of the dominant society as the "caretakers" of Deaf people. By professing to take care of Deaf people, the dominant society held them up to the standards of normality. In doing so, the dominant society affirmed the right to take away Deaf people's sign language. The strategy of the crucifixion declared that rather than "taking care" of Deaf people, the dominant structure oppressed and confined them. The rhetoric of confinement was also a strategy to jar Deaf people into the realization that they did not have to accept such oppressive impositions.

The theme of confinement is so pervasive a sentiment in the Deaf community that it persists even today. Deaf artist Betty G. Miller has expressed this perspective in her artwork. One of her creations, *Ameslan Prohibited,* portrays a powerful rhetorical statement in the form of a pair of broken hands constrained by handcuffs. Ella Mae Lentz, an ASL poet, eloquently expresses the deeply felt resentment of the Deaf community toward the dominant hearing society in her poem "The Door" (1995). The first stanza, in particular, exemplifies the crucifixion theme.

> We were simply talking in our language of signs
> When stormed by anthem-driven soldiers
> Pitched a fever by the score of their regime.
> They cuffed our hands, strangled us with iron reins.
> "Follow me! Line up! Now sit!"
> The captain, whip in hand,
> Inflicts his sentence with this command:
> Speak!
>
>   "Sh—?"
> Speak!
>
>   "—i—?"
> Speak!
>
>   "—t?"
> Damn your chains!
> We'll pronounce our own deliverance
> And articulate our message loud and clear.
>
> And for the width of a breath
> We grant each other asylum
> Talking in our language of signs.

When they pound, pound, pound.
"Don't answer. Don't open. It's bad, don't."
The thunder rolls again.
"But I want to. I want to see.
Well maybe. I just want to see."
So step by step we succumb

Our silent agreement undone.

Come out of your dark and silent world
And join us in our bright and lovely world.

Look! Those whose ears work are signing!
Yes, but such queer speech they shape.
What waits out there?
To be fair we should see more.
Could it be they've rearranged the score?

And one by one
We go down the corridor of their sterile syntax,
Not knowing . . .

Indeed, Deaf people emphasized the concept of sign language as their salvation by featuring sign language as an ideograph to represent the heart of their oppression.[4] One strategy was to document sign language in a form that would enable it to retain as permanent a status as possible. Some of these artifacts remain as lasting mementos in today's society.

One example is an icon in the form of the landmark statue of Thomas Hopkins Gallaudet and Alice Cogswell located at Gallaudet University. Deaf people raised funds to create the statue, and upon its completion, presented it in 1889 to Edward Miner Gallaudet, then president of the university, in honor of his father. Today the statue is listed as one of our national treasures. The statue signifies a permanent statement of the salvation that sign language brought to Deaf people. So important is sign language as a symbol of salvation that it carried over to the person who was perceived as responsible for bringing sign language to Deaf people. That person was Thomas Gallaudet, who is featured on the statue as teaching the alphabet to Alice, his first Deaf student. Alice's stance, which shows her standing next to Gallaudet, gazing up adoringly at him, embodies the view of Gallaudet as the savior of Deaf people.

Another strategy to preserve sign language took into account the visual nature of Deaf people. George Veditz, the seventh

The statue of Thomas Hopkins Gallaudet and Alice Cogswell was commissioned by the National Association of the Deaf and was presented to the National Deaf-Mute College (now Gallaudet University) in 1889.

Still frames from George Veditz's film *Preservation of the Sign Language,* in which he declares that sign language is the salvation of Deaf people.

president of the National Association of the Deaf (NAD), was the brainchild behind a series of films that included Veditz's own fiery delivery in the *Preservation of the Sign Language.* The film was created in 1913 as a strategy to reach Deaf constituents. In an era of increasing oralism, it was becoming more and more necessary to warn Deaf people of their fate. As such, the films were a consciousness-raising technique.[5]

Veditz's own film went one step further and employed rhetoric that posited sign language as a gift from a supreme being. Veditz declared that sign language was "the noblest gift God has given to Deaf people" (Veditz 1913). The reference to God's "noblest gift" is consequential because of the implication that God had created sign language, rather than the people themselves. And if God had created sign language, then Deaf people were simply putting God's "gift" to excellent use. Further, if God had created sign language, then sign language opponents thus cast into the role of the enemy must be the Devil's cronies. The implication here was that as God-fearing people, Deaf people should indeed seek salvation in their sign language.

This film project sponsored by the NAD from 1910 to 1920 took advantage of the unique network created by Deaf people. Consequently, Veditz and the NAD were able to circulate the films throughout the Deaf community, which included twenty-nine cities, twenty-seven conventions, and fifty-six schools for the Deaf (Schuchman 1988). Veditz's strategy was then an ideal way to stimulate Deaf audiences. Most important, he succeeded in his plan to preserve sign language, for his film, as well as several others, continues to be a rich source of study today.

In 1918, J. Schuyler Long contributed to the strategy of preserving sign language by authoring one of the earliest sign language books, *The Sign Language: A Manual of Signs*. With this book, Long was also able to offer to the Deaf social movement two other rhetorical strategies. One of these strategies was to call sign language a "language." Even though Deaf people did not have the necessary linguistic analyses at their disposal, and sign language was constantly demeaned as a substandard form of communication, Long proceeded to ascribe dignity to sign language. He explained that sign language exhibited some of the same features as other languages, such as arbitrariness and local dialect. By presenting sign language as a "beautiful and expressive language" and a "live" one, Long gave it validity (p. 19).

The other strategy Long used was to explain that "mouthing" was a "habit [that] is to be strongly condemned" (19). Rather than saying "oralism," he chose to use "mouthing." This approach moved sign language away from the throes of oralism, signifying its difference in modality and language. By isolating sign language from oralism, this strategy was a rebuff to attempts to control sign language, and a strategy to herald "muteness." In addition, by condemning any form of mouth movement, Long hoped to preserve sign language in its natural form without any undue influence from other languages.

By taking steps to preserve sign language, Deaf people in these times documented as fully as possible the importance of sign language in their lives. All the artifacts discussed in this section remain today and present a strong sense of the role of sign language in holding the Deaf community together. That these artifacts have endured over the years symbolizes the longevity of sign language and the Deaf community, despite outside intrusions.

Conclusion

The significance of this historical movement is in the emergence of the rhetorical "No." The rhetorical "No" marks the beginnings of a social movement. For the Deaf community, the historical movement signified a call for the end to the domination, condemnation, and correction of Deaf people. It was a rebellion against the dominant construct of "normality." The early Deaf social movement ferociously battled against the attempts to convert their community. Also, however, the early empowering strategies often centered around turning the dominant society's rhetorical practices to their advantage.

The "dividing practices" of the dominant structure, which at first isolated Deaf people from society, for instance, proved to be a saving grace for Deaf people. The establishment of a "class" of Deaf people enabled them to create a social structure in which organizations, newspapers, and intermarriages primarily involving Deaf people became a way of life. Not only was it a way of life, it became something Deaf people dearly cherished. At the heart of this "separate" community was sign language. The significance of this "class" of Deaf people was the empowering force of establishing a community of Deaf people with a distinctive means of communication that has prevailed despite all odds, even today.

During the era when the dominant society reversed itself and enforced oralism and integration, this strategy, however, threatened to destroy the way of life that Deaf people revered. Deaf people were not willing to sit passively by to watch this destruction of their community and their sign language. It was then necessary for them to develop strategies to counter the takeover of their community. Since sign language was the glue that bound Deaf people together, especially since it represented their chief means of communication and was not one shared with society, many of their strategies were developed to preserve sign language. Deaf people wanted to ensure that their sign language would not fade away. Since the dominant culture thought it their mission to take care of Deaf people, empowerment would not be an achievable goal for Deaf people within the dominant hierarchy. Consequently, if Deaf people wanted to empower themselves and guarantee their self-governance, it would be necessary to protect their community.

Taking action to preserve sign language became one way to protect their turf. The creation of a new hierarchy that posited hearing people at the bottom would also make it difficult for hearing people to dominate Deaf people within the Deaf community. The establishment of formal organizations such as the New England Gallaudet Association and the NAD also created a space for Deaf people to institute a network and to provide a safe haven in which to collaborate on injustices against them.

These strategies were effective in that many of these artifacts and organizations are still in existence today. Most significantly, sign language, even if not in its original form, remains at the heart of the Deaf community. Even as the dominant society succeeded in passing resolutions to take away sign language from educational institutions and attempted to strip all dignity from it, they could not completely eradicate sign language, nor could they dismantle the Deaf community. Aside from the basic human need to communicate and maintain social community, the strategies of the early Deaf movement garnered power for the community by turning the symbol of their oppression—sign language—into a symbol of their unity.

Notes

1. The publications of Deaf people were based on written English. However, as Jacques Derrida argues, the written text is a separate code from speech (1976). Although the written document may be based on the same linguistic structure as speech, writing requires from the author different skills than does speech from the speaker. This phenomenon is found in many speech communities that do not have an equivalent written form, such as the Navajo who speak in Navajo and write in English (Saville-Troike 1989). Thus, the assumption that written English is a form of "recorded" speech is merely a normalizing strategy to perpetuate the superiority of speech.

Further, Derrida argues for the superiority of written text as "enduring," versus that of speech as "ephemeral." Even so, as Adolf Hitler demonstrated, people are moved more by the spoken word than by the written word, and most movements are stimulated by great speakers, rather than writers (Duncan 1962). In this vein, the Deaf community revered sign language in face-to-face communication. However, in order to maintain opportunities for discourse and to record events conducted in sign language, written documents in English were needed.

2. So pervasive is this phenomenon that a deeper focus will commence in another chapter of this book.

3. William Jennings Bryan, a masterful orator and four-time presidential candidate, also made excellent use of this strategy. One of his most famous speeches, the "Cross of Gold," was delivered at the 1896 Democratic convention. During that speech, Bryan argued that America's economic system was in trouble unless it endeavored to substitute silver for the "cross of gold."

4. An ideograph is a symbol of what an object represents, rather than what it actually is. Michael McGee, a communications scholar, goes on to explain that an ideograph is culture-bound in which symbols "define a collectivity, i.e., the outer parameters of a society, because such terms either do not exist in other societies or do not have precisely similar meanings" (McGee 1980, 8). In this vein, sign language is an ideograph that has a shared meaning within the Deaf community and does not have the same meaning in the dominant culture.

5. Consciousness-raising is usually explained as a process in which face-to-face interaction provides opportunities for members of minority groups to analyze the nature and causes of their "oppression," which then becomes the basis for "revolutionary acts to eliminate oppression" (Sarachild 1970, 80). This often results in a sense of kinship in which members perceive other members as part of a "cultural family" or "community" (Chesebro, Cragan, and McCullough 1981, 211). Although the Deaf community did not use consciousness-raising groups in the way more contemporary groups such as the women's movement have used them, the film in this case served as the next-best thing. During this era, travel was not as convenient or as accessible as it is today, therefore, a film that could be transported from place to place was the most feasible option.

4

The Political Forces of the 1960s and 1970s

The early years of the Deaf social movement brought out ideological tensions: the dominant society sought first to segregate Deaf people from society, then to integrate them into the mainstream. The impact of dominant discourses was evident in the reign of oral domination in the education of Deaf people for more than seventy-five years. Members of the Deaf community remained active throughout this period: they were successful in establishing their own insurance company so that Deaf people could buy life insurance; they fought against legislation that prevented Deaf people from driving automobiles; and they continued to build community by establishing their own churches and organizations. But it was not until the 1960s that the Deaf community began once again to play an active role in strengthening their cultural identity in schools for the Deaf.

The era of the 1960s and 1970s presented a shift in context for the Deaf social movement. Two factors marked that shift. One was that the movement responded to the significant role played by the other liberating movements of the era. The second factor was the political impact of the other liberating movements: the dominant society enacted legislation to reduce discrimination against nondominant groups. For the Deaf social movement, this trend demanded a response to legislation to promote the integration of Deaf people into society. While the context of the early Deaf social movement involved the struggle between the Deaf community and the dominant society, the later phase of the movement presented a more complicated set of circumstances. Not

67

only did the Deaf social movement have to struggle against dominant discourses, it also had to do so within the context of the
rhetoric of other movements. Although benefiting from the attention given to the other movements, the Deaf movement had to
work with contrasting rhetorical positions that distinguished it
from other liberating movements.

The Deaf social movement simultaneously struggled against
dominant discourses that marginalized it and sought to retain the
benefits of the other movements' rhetoric while extricating itself
from the traps in their rhetoric. The Deaf social movement reacted
by presenting the Deaf community as a unique cultural and linguistic group deserving of a distinctive status.

Two Ideological Foes at War:
To Integrate or to Preserve Cultural Identity?

Most social movements share the characteristic of oscillating between "integrationist" and "nationalist" (or the preservation of
cultural identity) positions (Adam 1987, 92). The social movement history of African Americans, Native Americans, Hispanic
Americans, women, and lesbians and gays, for instance, indicates
such struggles. As a case in point, for African Americans, this
struggle marked the division between the civil rights and Black
Power movements. Proponents of the civil rights movement, the
integrationists, based their rhetoric on the democratic ideal that
"all men are created equal" and thus, as Americans, they should
also have an equal stake in achieving the American dream. As
Martin Luther King, Jr., probably the best-known advocate of
the "integrationist" ideology, declared in his "I Have a Dream"
speech in 1963, "All men would be guaranteed the unalienable
rights of life, liberty, and the pursuit of happiness" (Oates 1982,
259). And the way to attain equal access for everyone was to
remove societal barriers such as forced segregation and racial discrimination.

Further, the goals for desegregation were possible only by
working within the dominant society. Martin Luther King, Jr.,

argued, for example: "To succeed in a pluralistic society . . . the Negro obviously needs organized strength, but that strength will only be effective when it is consolidated through constructive alliances with the majority group" (King 1967, 50). The dilemma of integrationist rhetoric is that it creates a position that validates the dominant social order, by indicting it only in terms of the denial of access.

Since full participation in the dominant society is sought through direct appeal to dominant values, the social order determines the terms of its access, and those who conform most to dominant interests are also the most likely to be granted access (Bourdieu 1990). In this vein, minimizing differences between the nondominant and dominant becomes a strategy to fully participate in the dominant structure. Since maintaining the "normal" is made possible by minimizing differences, the results of the civil rights movement inadvertently stabilized the status quo.

The ideology of the Black Power movement took the opposite stance. As King pointed out: "Black Power is an implicit and often explicit belief in black separatism" (King 1967, 47). Stokely Carmichael, a proponent of separatism, explained the concept:

> We must organize black community power to end these abuses, and to give the Negro community a chance to have its needs expressed. A leadership which is truly "responsible"—not to the white press and power structure, but to the community—must be developed. Such leadership will recognize that its power lies in the unified and collective strength of that community. This will make it difficult for the white leadership group to conduct its dialogue with individuals in terms of patronage and prestige, and will force them to talk to the community's representatives in terms of real power. (Carmichael 1966, 650)

Indeed, the Black Power movement took the position not only that separatism paved the way toward "a sense of identity and pride in black people," but that integration led to the denial of "one's heritage, one's own culture" (Hamilton 1968, 22). Where the integrationists sought to minimize differences with the dominant culture, the separatists aspired to maximize the differences.

So too, has the women's movement encountered internal tensions between integrationist and separatist ideological factions. The integrationist wing of the women's movement is evident in the rhetoric of liberal feminists, or integrationists, who decry discrimination based on gender and seek equality under the U.S. Constitution. The proposal of the Equal Rights Amendment characterizes the position that recognizing women as equals will reduce disparities between women and men in all respects.

Separatist ideology within the women's movement, on the other hand, is represented by "cultural feminists" who stress differences between women and men and posit the qualities of women as sources of personal strength and pride (Donovan 1985, 31). Another form of separatism evident within both the women's and lesbians' social movements is the symbolic grouping of "political lesbians," which includes both lesbians and nonlesbians (Adam 1987, 93). The term is a political statement to declare a bonding against "male tyranny" and to "rescue women's culture from male domination" (94).

As the energy of the Deaf social movement reappeared in the late 1960s, these other liberation movements formed a background against which the rhetorical battles of the Deaf movement would be fought. The tensions of the other movements—integrationist versus separatist—would also mark divisions in efforts to address the suppression of Deaf people. One issue that followed this pattern centered around the role of language in the education and social community of Deaf people. Another dealt with the choice of turning energies toward political change rather than cultural identity and unity.

Strengthening Deaf Identity: Demarginalizing the Language of the Deaf Community

As a bonding force, the language of a group often becomes the symbol of its unity.[1] As such, languages, especially "spoken" (or signed) languages also distinguish one group from another.[2] Human beings are born with an innate need to reach out and interact with other people. Through the mechanism of language, people sustain relationships with one another. Language also creates and reinforces boundaries uniting people within a specific community and excluding outsiders (Saville-Troike 1989). "Spoken" languages represent a medium of expression in everyday discourse. For the Deaf community, the equivalent of the "spoken" is the "signed," and the language used by the Deaf community in the United States is American Sign Language (ASL).

To illustrate the tensions between the integrationist and culturalist factions in regard to language issues, this section will examine the response of the separatists, particularly of the African American movement, to the subjugation of their dialect (as a point of clarification, Black English is referred to as a "dialect," a "subsystem of the English language" [Smitherman 1989, 296–97]; it is considered an "*Africanized* [emphasis added] form of English," not merely a dialect of English [Smitherman 1977, 3]). These various ideologies exhibit similarities with regard to the tensions experienced in bringing about change, although the Deaf social movement has aimed to avoid the trap created by its distinctive rhetorical situation, which is similar to, yet different from, these other liberating movements.

Nondominant Discourses: Friend or Foe?

Separatists argue for the place of a common and distinct language as a form of identity to justify their efforts to maintain the diverse discourses of marginalized groups. Such groups—African Americans, Hispanic Americans, women, and Deaf people, among others—maintain distinctive discourses, they argue, even while living within a society that shares a dominant language. Their position is that the retention of their cultural identities adds to, rather than subtracts from, the well-being of marginalized members. They argue that discourses other than the dominant language are not inferior or substandard. Rather, they are separate languages that enable marginalized groups "to identify themselves and their place in the universe, as well as to permit them to communicate with one another about their unique social realities" (Samovar and Porter 1991, 159).

Many proponents of the culturalist stance present language as a tool of oppression against marginalized groups (Smitherman 1977). Researcher Robin Lakoff attests to the power of language: "Language is a change-creating force and therefore to be feared and used . . . not unlike fire" (Lakoff 1990, 13). Consequently, African American separatists, for instance, rebuff rhetoric that espouses the conformity to dominant standards as the road to self-sufficiency—rather, it paves the way to tokenism and co-optation.

African American separatists such as Geneva Smitherman (1977) have pointed out that the high rate of unemployment among college graduates—both African American and white—indicates that speaking standard English does not necessarily guarantee economic empowerment. More significantly, they argue, Black English is not detrimental to communicative competence, as speaking correctly does not equate to speaking well. Additionally, the preservation of Black English is desirable because it conveys thoughts and feelings different from those of standard English (J. Jordan 1981). As such, requiring conformity to standard English not only represses the voice of African Americans, but devalues the substance of their speech. The strategy of ignoring and/or denigrating the dialect of African Americans, as well as other marginalized groups, has served to cultivate an intolerance for differences because they represent the "abnormal." As such, this is a strategy of power in that the norm that heralds standard English continues to prevail and to limit access to a select few.

Smitherman ties this position to the importance of cultural diversity: teaching Black English in school not only to African American children, but also to their white peers can defuse the pervasive linguistic and cultural snobbery of Americans (1977). Further, multicultural education in schools can generate a tolerance not only of African Americans, but also of differences in general. The reasoning of African Americans that multicultural education not only assists in the preservation of their cultural identities, but leads to a more accepting stance toward cultures persuaded at least one state to recognize Black English. In 1979 Michigan courts acknowledged that Black English is a separate dialect from standard English and further required that schools take this into consideration when teaching African American students (J. Jordan 1981).

Almost twenty years later, in December 1996, a new controversy arose when the Oakland, California, school district became the first school system in the United States to recognize Black English, or Ebonics, as a language. This decision was made "to improve the chronically poor grades of many black students in Oakland's public schools by acknowledging that their language habits are rooted in a distinct culture and that they may need special help to learn standard English" (Sanchez 1996, A8). This move by the Oakland school board touched off a storm of rhetoric for and against this approach. William Labov, a linguistics researcher who has studied Black English, faults the lack of understanding of Ebonics to the "emotional reactions" it evokes, citing that "it's such a politically loaded situation" (Sanchez 1997, A1). The Oakland policy proved so controversial that within a month after establishing the policy, the school board voted to remove references to Ebonics as "genetically based" and "the primary language" of many African Americans (Ebonics Plan Altered 1997, A6). This struggle bears close resemblance to conflicts in the Deaf community over ASL as the "native language" vs. "one of many languages" of Deaf people.

Integrationists adopt the stance that the retention of marginalized languages in a dominant culture where the language of access is English presents a dilemma for marginalized groups wishing to fully participate in the public sphere. Retaining one's nondominant language is detrimental to marginalized peoples because it "excludes them from full participation in the world we live in" (R. L. Jones 1989, 308). As writer Richard Rodriguez explains, holding on to the nondominant culture and language excludes one from being an American and from full participation in that society: "Only when I was able to think of myself as an American, no longer an alien in gringo society, could I seek the rights and opportunities necessary for full public individuality" (Rodriguez 1989, 251). The preservation of distinct languages "impairs" the acquisition of the dominant language and, thus, the participation of marginalized people in the public sphere. Although integrationists posited nondominant discourses as a barrier to achieving the American dream, the existence of various distinct languages that continue to bond their respective groups also threatens the stability of the status quo. These distinctive cultural identities that share languages other than that of the dominant language are then deemed as inimical to the "norm," in that they do not retain the values and ideals of the social order.

This rhetoric—arguing that the use of nondominant languages creates barriers to the dominant structure for marginalized members—established a hierarchy ranking the standard language superior to nondominant languages. The dominant language then became a norm and language differences, deviations from that norm. Consequently, integrationist rhetoric turned nondominant languages into a rhetoric of deficiency. This practice is illustrated in the following characterizations of people using speech patterns such as "I is, you is," and "I ain't, you ain't": these "mark the user as belonging definitely outside the pale of cultivated, educated society" and its users are "illiterate or uncultivated" (Pooley 1989, 280). Thus, embracing a diversity of languages is perceived as jeopardizing the American identity. By presenting standard English as *the* language and the *standard,* dominant discourses could legitimize the necessity of conforming to the norm.

The women's movement has faced a similar struggle to legitimize women's ways of speaking. As Deborah Tannen, author of the best-selling *You Just Don't Understand: Women and Men in Conversation,* explains, men speak from the framework of "status" and "independence," and women speak a language of "connection" and "intimacy" (1990). The integrationist stance perceives men's speech as the language of power. Such discourse is authoritative and is, thus, granted permission to dictate public, economic, and social decisions. Women's ways of speaking, in comparison, are powerless and ineffective if women want to succeed in the public sphere. Women had to become more assertive and abandon powerless forms of talk in order to achieve access to the dominant society. In short, the integrationist position maintains that the emulation of male forms of talk would grant women success in a male-dominated society.

The tendency in more recent times has been, however, to portray women's and men's ways of talking as different, rather than as inferior and superior. As writer Barrie Thorne puts it, the language patterns of women and men represent "two alien cultures, oddly intertwined" (Pfeiffer 1989, 205). By rejecting the subjugated status placed on women's language patterns in integrationist rhetoric, the difference position values the unique discourse of women. The unique discourse of women is imbedded in the central role of gender differences and its impact on individual identity. In foregoing that part of themselves by imitating men's language patterns, women invalidate themselves. Tannen's work supports this position.

Consequently, the growing awareness of the subjugated placement of marginalized discourses has warranted a battle for the legitimization of these forms of language. As African Americans and women have fought for the recognition of their unique language patterns, so too has the Deaf movement gotten on the bandwagon.

The Deaf Social Movement Rekindles the Ashes

Although the struggles over communication issues were not new for Deaf people, the battles begun by the liberating movements created a new rhetorical context for the Deaf social movement. The most obvious difference between the liberating movements and the Deaf movement in the struggle to liberate marginalized discourses was the modality of the discourse. African American and women's languages share a commonality with dominant languages, in that all are spoken. That the Deaf community communicates in a modality other than speech presents an issue not evident in the other movements.

Prior to the era of the liberating movements, the Deaf community had been subject to oral domination for years. During this era, ASL was forbidden in classrooms. Deaf students were severely penalized if they were caught signing—their hands were slapped or they were forced to sit on their hands. However, ASL had continued to persevere and grow throughout the years. Residential schools for the Deaf provided this avenue, although signing was, for the most part, forbidden in the classroom. During these years, many Deaf students went home only during winter and summer vacations. For these students, the dormitory was their home. And the dormitory was the central place for the transmission of their language and culture. ASL was used in the dormitory and passed on from generation to generation.

After years of suppression of ASL in the classroom, the advent of the liberating movements presented the Deaf community with a rhetorical opportunity to reinstate sign language in the classroom. They also, however, faced an integrationist faction that demanded conformity to speech as a means of access to the dominant society. Unlike the other liberating movements, the Deaf community's response to this conflict was to compromise. The aspect of sign language as a polar opposite to the spoken language created a means for compromise not available to the other movements.

The compromise strategy proposed by the Deaf movement to bring sign language back into the classroom was "total communication." Total communication is a philosophy, rather than a "method," that endorses individual communication rights. In other words, any and all modes of communication, including sign language, speech and speechreading, reading and writing, among others, may be used in the instruction of Deaf students. Since total communication was a philosophy that purported to embrace speech as well as sign language, it served to placate both the integrationists and separatists. Precisely because total communication retained the integrationist theme of access to the dominant public sphere, the Deaf community was able to sell the implementation of total communication to educational institutions still dominated by integrationists. The community went on record as not opposing speech training, but attributed little value to the practice. Author Leo Jacobs was typical in observing that the acquisition of speech skills was not "a matter of life or death" to Deaf people (Jacobs 1974, 15).

Even as the Deaf social movement endorsed total communication, Deaf people reversed the stress: where dominant discourses placed the greatest significance of total communication on speech, Deaf people elevated sign language as the most important. Dominant discourses accepted total communication in which sign language would "*reinforce* [emphasis added] speechreading and audition" (Denton 1972, 55). Deaf people such as Leo Jacobs reversed the status: "the use of total communication, or rather, free expression with the manual communication sector of total communication" (Jacobs 1974, 48).

The strategy of total communication succeeded because it placated the greatest number of people with diverse ideologies. Opposing ideologies were able to take comfort in total communication since they could glean their own interpretations of the philosophy. Consequently, a majority of educational institutions for Deaf students adopted the policy of total communication in their programs. By 1978, 65 percent of schools and programs educating Deaf children had converted to total communication (I. K. Jordan, Gustason, and Rosen 1979).

Once total communication had legitimized the use of sign language in schools, the opportunity was then available for Deaf students to assert more control in the classroom. This opportunity began with the stark comparison of the two modes. Because schools were still very much dominated by the patriarchal system, educators adopted integrationists' modalities to prepare Deaf children for entrance to the dominant society, anywhere from the use of speech only to speech reinforced by some code of signed English (Woodward, Allen, and Schildroth 1988). However, studies began to multiply which illustrated the incompatibility of these systems with the visual nature of Deaf children (Baker 1978; Crandall 1974; Erting 1982; Johnson, Liddell, and Erting 1989; Kluwin 1981; Marmor and Petitto 1979; Quigley and Paul 1984). In addition, many teachers came to the classroom with low levels of competence in sign language (Crittendon 1986). As a result, Deaf students frequently found themselves frustrated in their efforts to learn within a system that often did not accommodate them. Thus, without declaring open warfare on the educational system, Deaf students exploited the opportunity for a strategy for co-optation within total communication, a strategy Genovese calls "resistance within accommodation"(1972).[3] Genovese illustrated how slaves resisted their masters without appearing to openly oppose them. Slaves broke machinery or faked illness to put their masters in a position of caring for them, along with other forms of resistance. Similar strategies by Deaf students paved the way toward the transformation of sign language into a symbol of power and cultural unity.

Consider an illustration of how Deaf students might use sign language as a strategy of symbolic control over oppressors. A new teacher with meager signing skills might ask Deaf students how to sign a particular word. Instead of demonstrating the appropriate sign, students might show the teacher an obscene sign. The unsuspecting teacher will continue to use the "new" sign, to gales of laughter each time it is used, until enlightened. When the Deaf students place the teacher, their unwitting confederate and stooge, into an inferior role, they place themselves in a superior position. This is the power of "inside" jokes—it excludes the outsider such as the teacher and thus creates cultural unity among insiders who understand the joke.

While total communication provided opportunities to locally legitimize the modality of sign language, the struggle to authenticize sign language—to achieve acknowledgment that sign language constituted a formal language on a par, yet separate from standard English—was an entirely different matter. Although Deaf people shared with other marginalized groups the subjugation of their language, other groups could achieve their objectives with their language interpreted as a variation of English. Deaf people uniquely faced the danger of their sign language being reduced to a mere different "mode" of expression.

Samovar and Porter explain that the languages of African Americans and women are "argots" (or dialects) (1991).[4] American Sign Language does not fall into the category of argot, nor is it a dialect of English. There are also differences in spoken and signed languages. Instead of the voice, signed languages use space to present signs and aspects of the body (the hands, eyes, head, and facial and upper body movements) to create a complex gestural-visual language (Baker 1983). The Deaf social movement was, thus, faced with the rhetorical predicament of benefiting from the struggle of the liberating movements to elevate the status of previously substandard discourses, yet doing so in a way that avoided the trap of allowing ASL to be categorized as a dialect of English. One strategy was to declare that ASL was indeed a bona fide "language." This strategy sought to place American Sign Language on a par with all other languages, most prominently English. Since dominant discourses so prevalently denigrated ASL as substandard, with its characterization of ASL as "concrete," "idiomatic," and "bad English," the constitution of ASL as a language created a sense of pride among Deaf people.

The Deaf social movement was able to point to research that began with William C. Stokoe's landmark work demonstrating that ASL is a rule-governed language with its own grammatical structure, morphology, and syntax (Klima and Bellugi 1979; Stokoe 1960; Woodward 1973, 1974). These characteristics mark ASL as a complete language, just like English, French, or German. Unlike most of the non-ethnic marginalized discourses in the United States, ASL shares more commonality in linguistic structure with Latin, Russian (Baker and Padden 1978), Navajo, and Japanese (Wilcox and Wilbers 1987), than with standard English.

However, it was not until twenty years later that Deaf discourses began to laud ASL as a language of their community, and it took another ten years for the Deaf social movement to promote its use in the classroom. A look at the prevailing discourses during the earlier years places this response from the Deaf community in its context. Researchers in recent years have begun to analyze the devastating effects of "audism" on Deaf people (Baker-Shenk 1986; Kannapell 1993; Lane 1992; Lane, Hoffmeister, and Bahan 1996; Nover 1995). *Audism* is a term coined by author Tom Humphries (1975) to refer, in a vein similar to racism, sexism, homophobia, and the various "isms," to the practice of paternalism and institutional discrimination toward Deaf people. So prevalent has the practice of audism in the education of Deaf people been, that it took years before Deaf people could embrace their community's language. In *The Mask of Benevolence: Disabling the Deaf Community,* author Harlan Lane argues that when the minority language is devalued or ignored, this results in a negative self-concept and serves to maintain the power structure of the majority culture (1992). As researcher Stephen M. Nover sums it up: "On the whole, over the last hundred years, English-only educators have successfully reproduced, maintained, and promoted auditory-based values and English-only beliefs within their own ranks. Consequently, they have had the capacity to maintain considerable control over Deaf people and modify their behaviors accordingly" (Nover 1995, 122–23). Nover has called this the process of "hearization." In fact, an influx of discourses to decry and condemn such practices has become a strategy of the Deaf movement, in keeping with the trend of other social movements to label practices of institutional discrimination. Examples of such rhetoric used by the Deaf movement to label these practices, in addition to audism and hearization, include the "English is intelligence" syndrome (Baker cited in Kannapell 1993, 15); "communication violence" (expounded on more fully in a later chapter); "ASL-as-problem" orientations (Nover 1995).

As the Deaf movement began to decry audism, coinciding with the advent of mounting research at their disposal, Deaf people like former NAD president Mervin D. Garretson were able to exalt: "To know once, and for all, that our 'primitive' and 'ideographic gestures' are really a formal language, on a par with all other languages of the world is a step towards pride and liberation" (Garretson 1980, vi). The rhetoric of "language" increased the stature of Deaf people by positing their language as a distinctive linguistic structure.

From the status created by their "low verbal" English language skills, ASL as language also transformed Deaf people into intelligent beings with not only one, but two languages at their disposal. Sociolinguist Barbara Kannapell describes the Deaf bilingual: "Ideally the deaf adult is a fluent signer of ASL and able to read and write the English language. . . . When he talks with deaf friends, he will use ASL. When he talks with hearing people he writes English on paper, or speaks through an interpreter, or uses his speech if it is intelligible enough" (Kannapell 1974, 10). The establishment of a "bilingual" identity for Deaf people confers the highest prominence on those who demonstrate fluency in two languages. ASL is the badge with which Deaf people are accepted as members of the Deaf community, suggesting that a Deaf person who is primarily monolingual in ASL will be better accepted in the Deaf community than by the dominant society. On the other hand, a Deaf person who uses primarily English will be better accepted in the dominant society than by the Deaf community.

However, for Deaf people to be bilingual, they are required to demonstrate English skills as well. This indicates the compromise position between integrationist and separatist discourse by placing a high value on both languages. Even so, those with the strongest Deaf identity are the most likely to be bilingual. Research has consistently shown that Deaf children of Deaf parents attain higher academic achievement scores than do Deaf children of hearing families (Stuckless and Birch 1966; Meadow 1968; Vernon and Koh 1970; Corson 1973; Brasel and Quigley 1977). Although not all Deaf parents use ASL or even sign language, the chances are higher that their Deaf children will acquire ASL skills, thereby building a strong foundation in which to learn English skills. Thus, the creation of the bilingual identity, even as it embraced the dominant language, was also exploited to give the highest prominence to the strongest Deaf identity, in most cases—Deaf children of Deaf parents.

The liberating movements and the attention focused on their struggle for cultural identification created a path that the Deaf social movement took advantage of. Even as total communication was a strategy of compromise, it was significant in promoting sign language as a visible force of the community. From a strategy of compromise, the movement moved to the stronger position of establishing ASL as language and Deaf people as bilingual. The rhetorical strategies to symbolize ASL promoted the Deaf identity and strengthened the Deaf social movement.

Strengthening the Deaf Identity: Reacting to Social-Engineering Practices

Along with the conflict over gaining access to the dominant society via the dominant language versus the preservation of marginalized discourses—integrationists also found themselves at odds with the separatists over legislative issues. The era of the liberating movements of the 1960s and 1970s resulted in a flurry of court decisions and legislative action. The civil rights movement, for example, was able to turn for support to court cases such as *Brown v. Board of Education* or to help bring about legislation such as the 1957, 1960, and 1964 civil rights mandates that sanctioned the integration of African Americans and women into the dominant society by prohibiting discrimination on the basis of race or sex. The early successes of these social movements thus paved the way for an emphasis on integration into American society for all dispossessed groups, including disabled people and Deaf people.

Integrationists helped enact these legislative actions based on the ideology that removing barriers to access promoted equal opportunity. After all, equality would be difficult to achieve in a predominantly white and racist society without legislation to monitor discriminatory practices that would otherwise persevere.

The rhetoric of integration was based on the belief that America was indeed the land of opportunity and freedom, although in practice this invitation was not extended to African Americans. Martin Luther King, Jr., makes this clear in his "I Have a Dream" speech:

> When the architects of our republic wrote the magnificent words of the Constitution and the Declaration of Independence, they were signing a promissory note to which every American was to fall heir. . . . It is obvious today that America has defaulted on this promissory note insofar as her citizens of color are concerned. Instead of honoring this sacred obligation, America has given the Negro people a bad check; a check which has come back marked "insufficient funds." But we refuse to believe that the bank of justice is bankrupt. . . . So we have come to cash this check—a check that will give us upon demand the riches of freedom and the security of justice. (Oates 1982, 259–60)

Because America had "defaulted" in her promise of the American dream to African Americans, legislation was deemed necessary to force America to pay up. The enforcement of integration into the dominant society was thus a means to ensure that African Americans would have the same opportunities as their European American counterparts to achieve a stake in the American dream. By removing barriers to access, the notable American ethic of ambition and hard work represents qualities that will put the American promise within reach of marginalized people.

To separatists, however, legislation that enforced integration in reality integrated only a few select nondominant members, rather than the marginalized group as a whole. Further, integration fostered the destruction of the cultural identity. Stokely Carmichael promoted such a viewpoint: "Its [integration's] goal was to make the white community accessible to 'qualified' Negroes and presumably each year a few more Negroes armed with their passports—a couple of University degrees—would escape into the middle-class America and adopt the attitudes and life styles of that group; and one day the Harlems and the Watts would stand empty, a tribute to the success of integration" (Carmichael 1966,

647). In effect, the dominant society would be interested only in "qualified" nondominant members. Since the dominant structure determined the terms of full participation in their society, those deemed "qualified" were individuals who demonstrated the most similarity to members of that society. As such, full participation in the dominant culture was granted to those who discarded their nondominant cultural identity in favor of the values and lifestyles of that culture. Separatist rhetoric thus posited that integration, rather than favoring the nondominant culture, recognized only those members who conformed to dominant standards. Consequently, legislation to integrate nondominant peoples into the dominant society not only failed for the marginalized group as a whole, but denigrated the uniqueness of nondominant cultures.

The tensions between integrationist and separatist rhetoric in the other liberating movements, as the dominant society moved in the direction of enacting legislative measures to reduce discriminatory practices, also marked the experience of the Deaf social movement.

Mainstreaming as Virtue: Responding to Charges of Discrimination

The rhetoric of "separate, but equal" educational facilities as discriminatory carried over to the Deaf community as well. This viewpoint is espoused by Diane Castle, wife of former National Technical Institute for the Deaf vice-president William C. Castle: "Many parents, educators, doctors, and audiologists recognize the competition Deaf persons will encounter in the work place and believe that preparation to enter the mainstream of society is the best educational approach" (Castle 1990, 19). Further, the best means of ensuring full participation was for Deaf people to emulate the behavior of their hearing peers. Castle goes on to say: "Deaf adults who have had the opportunity to develop spoken and written English, speechreading and listening skills have the greatest opportunity for entering challenging employment and gaining good promotions. . . . [M]ost deaf people need to choose to be part of the mainstream and to integrate within the larger society" (21). This integrationist rhetoric confirms the belief that America is, indeed, full of opportunities, but only for those who adapt to society.

Castle echoes the integrationist theme that ambition and hard work are individualistic endeavors that pave the way to successful integration. Castle's argument additionally implies that all Deaf people have at their disposal the ability to develop "spoken," "speechreading," and "listening" skills. Further, mainstreaming in schools provides the best means with which to ensure that Deaf children interact with hearing children and thus increase the opportunity for eventual integration into society.

Since the mainstreaming of disabled children, and therefore Deaf children, into public schools played upon the integrationist goal of providing them with access to the dominant society, legislation was deemed necessary to promote institutional enforcement of mainstreaming. Behind this push for legislation were parents of disabled children, primarily mentally retarded children, who had historically been excluded from public schools. Proclaimed the Education for all Handicapped Children Act of 1975 (now renamed the Individuals with Disabilities Education Act), Public Law 94-142 requires that disabled students be taught in the "least restrictive environment." Dominant discourses often interpret the "least restrictive environment" to mean the placement of disabled children into classrooms with nondisabled children. By placing disabled children into the mainstream of the dominant society, integrationists offered a form of "equal opportunity." In reality, however, disabled children were often placed in separate classes for disabled children in the same school building as their nondisabled peers, which only continued the practice of a "separate" education. Dissatisfaction with this "partial" integration led to the current "full inclusion" movement, in which disabled students are expected to participate as equals in classrooms with nondisabled students (Shapiro 1994).

Responding to Social-Engineering Practices:
The Deaf Cultural Community

To the Deaf social movement, "mainstreaming" or "inclusion" did not necessarily pave the way to "equal opportunity." Rather, separatist rhetoric painted "mainstreaming" as averse to the identity and well-being of Deaf children. Mervin Garretson argued:

> Deaf children may find themselves cast adrift without much of a self-identity because they are compelled to settle for half a life in a hearing community that is only partially accessible to them. When they finally reach their late teens and leave school as young adults and are forced to wrestle with these realities, they will seek out the deaf community. But the process of enculturation and adaptation to a new language is not easy. All too frequently, they wind up not fully accepted by either the deaf or hearing community. (Schein 1989, 143)

The response to legal enforcement of "mainstreaming" Deaf children into public schools and the categorization of Deaf people as "disabled" was to create a discourse that reversed the value of mainstreaming for the Deaf community and constructed new images to detract from the pathological definition of "disability."

Deaf people soon discovered that Public Law 94-142 created a rhetorical dilemma for them. The Deaf social movement found that it needed to address the fact that this new law created more problems than opportunities for Deaf students. The movement pointed to the Amy Rowley case as an example of dominant practices that created barriers to full participation. The case of *The Board of Education of the Hendrick Hudson Central School District v. Rowley*, 458 U.S. 176 (1982), was the first to reach the Supreme Court in response to Public Law 94-142. Amy was a Deaf student who was "mainstreamed" and was doing well. However, her parents argued that since she was understanding only 59 percent of what was said in the classroom, that she would benefit optimally with an interpreter present. Although lower courts ruled that she was not receiving an appropriate education without an interpreter, the Supreme Court reversed the decision. Their contention was that the intent of the law was simply to provide access, not to "maximize" each child's capability (Geer 1986).

The Individuals with Disabilities Education Act (IDEA), as PL 94-142 is now called, has been left to interpretation by a wide variety of educational authorities. As long as the state policy does not violate the federal law, placement decisions can be made by state courts; by state education agencies and local education agencies; by Department of Education policies; by state regulations and policies; and by individuals, including school district administrators, superintendents, teachers, and parents. In practice, this has meant that placement decisions are often made at the whim of the ideological framework of the persons involved in the decision-making process, regardless of what may be in the best interests of the particular student. Integrationist rhetoric, playing on the promotion of "equal opportunity" has been very effective in the current push for full inclusion. As a result, large numbers of Deaf children are currently attending public schools rather than residential schools. Prior to the 1960s, almost 80 percent of Deaf children attended residential schools; in contrast, only about 30 percent currently attend residential schools (Lane, Hoffmeister, and Bahan 1996). In the face of inclusionist rhetoric, "segregation" became the adversary. It was thus necessary to attempt to eradicate residential schools, for they represented the antithesis of full inclusion. As a result, in some states, residential schools for the Deaf were threatened with shutdowns.

In reaction to social-engineering practices that, for instance, threatened to shut down residential schools, local communities of Deaf people frequently rallied to preserve their schools. The residential school became a symbol of separatist rhetoric. After all, separatists argued, residential schools meant much more to Deaf people than simply a place to acquire an education. For many Deaf people, the residential school was where they learned sign language, were able to interact freely with peers, and most significantly, where they became encultured into the community of Deaf people. Thus, the preservation of residential schools symbolized the sustenance of the Deaf community, whereas mainstreaming represented its destruction.

Once mainstreaming, a symbol of destruction for the Deaf community, became legally sanctioned, separatists presented mainstreaming as a force antithetical to the development of the Deaf identity. Along with the other separatist movements, the Deaf movement sought to maintain the identity of their community. The Deaf community thus targeted mainstreaming, now called inclusion, and called upon the resources of its language as a way to build community within the contemporary rhetorical spectacle. The Deaf social movement adopted strategies to maintain residential schools, and to condemn mainstreaming and full inclusion as a symbol of their oppression. One such strategy is the use of humor. An example is a joke by humorist Lynn Jacobowitz: "How do you prevent mainstreaming programs? Blow up public schools." While this joke may seem unduly harsh, it represents the attitude of many Deaf people toward mainstreaming. When mainstreaming is depicted as the annihilation of the Deaf community, "blowing up" public schools can be viewed as an equivalent destruction, a form of self-defense.

As a strategy, humor offers a way to illuminate the inequalities inherent in society and can simultaneously function as a catalyst for social change (Arnez and Anthony 1968). The use of humor not only allows marginalized groups to temporarily poke fun at their oppressors and gain the upper hand, it also releases tensions by allowing them to challenge their oppressors on a symbolic level (Douglas 1968). As such, the strategy of humor enables humorists like Jacobowitz to challenge the social order by illuminating mainstreaming as a form of oppression. Implicit in her joke is the portrayal of Deaf people as victims and dominant society as oppressors. The joke is then a "safe" way to draw attention to what is perceived as a very real oppressive situation. The shock value of the joke also transforms humor into a jarring consciousness of the harsh realities of mainstreaming. By establishing a

The traditional sign for *mainstreaming* symbolizes integration into the dominant society.

The transformed sign for *mainstreaming* symbolizes the Deaf person's isolation and domination by hearing society.

"we" against "them" dichotomy, the joke helps to bond the Deaf community and subsequently to resist impositions against them.

Separatist rhetoric also rejects the dominant construct of mainstreaming by creating a discourse of mockery. This is achieved by transforming the dominant position of mainstreaming as opportunity into mainstreaming as a symbol of oppression. The rhetoric of mockery is embodied in the transformation of the traditional sign for mainstreaming. The traditional sign reinforces the perception that mainstreaming equals integration, with an illustration of many Deaf people equally placed with many hearing people. Inherent in this perception is the myth that once Deaf people are placed among their hearing peers, they will learn to read and write English fluently, to speak and hear (by using hearing aids or similar devices)—and by all accounts, become successfully integrated.

To repudiate this myth, another sign for mainstreaming was created in mockery: an image of only one Deaf person in the midst

The Deaf community created a sign
for *inclusion* that clearly illustrates
their renunciation of this concept.

of a mass of hearing people, and the Deaf person is subordinately
squashed underneath the mob of hearing people. Inherent in this
characterization is the substitution of the myth of mainstreaming
as a barrier to discrimination for the reality of mainstreaming as
discrimination.

As the rhetoric of full inclusion came into being, separatist
rhetoric mocked this concept as well. As the tension mounted
between foes of full inclusion and supporters of residential
schools for the Deaf, separatist discourses became even more bla-
tant. To illustrate their abhorrence of full inclusion, the Deaf
movement retaliated with a sign for inclusion that represented an
image of a Deaf student being placed out of sight, in a dark,
remote corner. However, while the Deaf movement privately rejects the full inclusion position, in public, a more moderate stance
is generally presented. As a case in point, while the National Association of the Deaf states in its position paper on full inclusion
that it **"does not support"** [boldface in original text] full inclusion, it also endorses an expansion of the "Full Continuum of
Alternative Placements" section of the IDEA (Position statement

on full inclusion 1994). Indeed, recent rhetoric has focused on the endorsement of a "continuum" of placements and the notion that placement decisions should be geared toward each individual student.

The creation of new discourses, as revealed in the mockery of the sign for mainstreaming and inclusion, is a symbolic condemnation of the dominant structure's social-engineering efforts. That the new symbols are expressed in the language of the Deaf community is a liberating strategy. Marginalized groups, because they are "suppressed" by a language structure not of their own creation, usually begin to express their ideas in the dominant language. Since the dominant language incorporates the experiences of the dominant culture, the experiences of marginalized groups are excluded.

Another strategy has been to posit inclusion as an evil force by calling it the equivalent of "cultural genocide." Poet Ella Mae Lentz embodies this notion in her signed poem "The Children's Garden." Colorful flowers represent Deaf children who are brought together because of their beauty. However, society cannot tolerate the beauty of these colorful flowers, wanting them to be "brown" like all the others, and thus it cuts off their roots and transplants them individually elsewhere. This represents society's desire to "deindividualize" Deaf children by integrating them with hearing children. However, without their "roots," they will wither and die.

The "cultural genocide" strategy exemplifies inclusion with a strenuousness that strengthens the we/they distinction, thereby fostering the unity of the Deaf community. When Lentz compares mainstreaming to a garden, Deaf children in mainstream programs symbolize the slow and wilting death of the flowers. The analogy represents the "death" of the Deaf identity and consequently of Deaf people. Such portraits of death conjure up powerful images that simultaneously strengthen the community, for they are "facing the same fate," and that encourage the movement to resist this fate.

Like the other strategies in this stage, the expressions of genocide in the poem show the Deaf movement describing injustices in their native language. Where previously Deaf artists were encouraged to express themselves via the dominant language of English, the new assertion of Deaf people as a linguistic group gave rise to artistic expression in ASL. Poets of ASL, such as Lentz, Clayton Valli, Patrick Graybill, and others have publicly declared this viewpoint. These poets often tell of how they struggled to express their poetry in English, but that true empowerment did not occur until they began to do so in their native language of ASL.

Thus, artistic demonstrations are significant in legitimizing public expression in ASL. The promotion of ASL as a language paved the way toward greater community acceptance and use of the language. With the acceptance of ASL as a medium in which to express injustices publicly, more Deaf people could be recruited to the cause of the Deaf social movement. By demonstrating inequalities in a medium that was more accessible to many Deaf people, the consciousness of a greater number of Deaf people would be raised.

Rhetorical strategies that reject inclusionist discourses, like creating jokes and signs to mock its meaning, and defining inclusion as "cultural genocide," are part and parcel of the process of empowerment for Deaf people. By developing their own rhetoric, Deaf people maintain a sense of control over themselves. As Paulo Freire notes, struggles can empower only when the dominated groups develop their own meanings and strategies (1970). Thus, with the creation of symbols within their own language structure, the Deaf movement not only communicated its ideology but also demonstrated the viability of its language. A new consciousness often gives rise to a new discourse. Foucault calls this the "insurrection of subjugated knowledges" (Foucault 1980, 81). The consciousness of a social movement grows and strengthens by creating redefinitions for existing terms, then advances its cause further by giving rise to a new discourse. Accordingly, the development of new discourse further bonds the Deaf community together and preserves its unity.

Demonstrating resistance to dominant discourses also enables the unveiling of the politics within the dominant rhetoric (Foucault 1978). Since social movement discourse was increasingly presented in the language of Deaf people, these symbolic entities could be transmitted into structural activities. Additionally, the promotion of collective action worked to preserve the Deaf community by providing a space for discourse and structural activity. The preservation of the Deaf community became evident in the transformation of rhetorical strategies, such as "cultural genocide," into action. For instance, in 1982 the British National Union of the Deaf formally charged their government with a violation of the United Nations Convention on the Prevention and Punishment of the Crime of Genocide (Lane 1985; Lee 1992). Their rationale was that "deaf schools are being effectively forced to close and therefore children of one ethnic/linguistic minority group, that is, deaf people, are being forcibly transferred to another group, that is, hearing people" (Lane 1985, 10). The rationale clearly distinguished the separatist position from the integrationist one. The separatists traded upon this differentiation, while the integrationists sought to eliminate it.

By declaring themselves a linguistic and cultural group, Deaf people now had a rhetorical tool with which to shed the prevalent pathological image of them. Although the separatists had adopted the label "disability" for political reasons, such as lobbying for legal rights for all disabled people, Deaf people do not usually identify themselves as disabled. As Padden and Humphries explain: " 'Disabled' is a label that historically has not belonged to Deaf people. . . . Deaf people have a history, albeit an uneasy one, of alignment with other disabled groups. . . . 'Disabled' is not a primary term of self-identification, indeed it is one that requires a disclaimer" (Padden and Humphries 1988, 44).

While the Deaf movement shares with the disability movement the common goal of repudiating discriminatory practices against their members, this is not a goal restricted to these groups. Dominant discourses have used the same strategies of labeling people who are perceived as different as lesser beings. Take the labels of "parasites" for Jewish people in Nazi Germany, "coons" for African Americans, "spics" for Hispanic Americans, "savages" for Native Americans, "chicks" for women, "fags" for gay men, and the list goes on. Because such labeling has often justified discriminatory practices against nondominant groups, many social movements have sought to redefine their communities, as have Deaf and disabled people. Therefore, the repudiation of discriminatory discourses in itself is insufficient to bind Deaf and disabled people together, for this is a strategy that has been adopted by virtually every marginalized movement.

Although Deaf people benefit from civil laws such as Section 504 of the Rehabilitation Act and the Americans with Disabilities Act, they perceive themselves as having more in common with other linguistic and cultural groups. Unlike the disabled community, Deaf people have a language and culture that binds them. More significantly, the disabled community is comprised of hearing people who have more in common with the general populace than they do with Deaf people. Let us for a minute put a Deaf person, a hearing person, and another hearing person with a wheelchair in the same room. The most likely pair to strike up a conversation would be the two hearing people. After all, they communicate by speaking and hearing, unlike most Deaf people. Accordingly, rather than affiliating with the disability movement, the Deaf movement has, for the most part, retained its separateness by redefining the Deaf community as a cultural group. This separateness is a critical distinction for the Deaf movement, which has a different goal from the disability movement. The disability movement seeks full integration into the community in all phases of life, from school to work. This goal is perceived as "cultural genocide" for the Deaf community, which celebrates its uniqueness as a cultural entity.

By projecting the image of a cultural entity, Deaf people could present themselves as "complete" persons. The medical model that had defined them as incomplete was now shunned because it had effectively depicted Deaf people as what Barbara Kannapell, a

Deaf sociolinguist, noted are pathologically "broken ears," rather than as human beings, and their method of communication as "disorders" rather than a real language. Others in the Deaf community brought visual attention to the "big ear" concept. Harry Williams and Clayton Valli created artistic works, the former in a painting, the latter in an ASL poem, simultaneously dramatizing and mocking the "big ear." These strategies mock the perception of Deaf people as having a medical condition. By exaggerating the size of the ear, the strategy challenges the dominant culture to deny their fascination with the "disorder of the ear." It also calls on Deaf people to reject the pathological and to reaffirm their cultural identity.

The Deaf community has reacted to the imposition of the "disability" label, not by proving their superiority to other disabled groups, but by defying the image of the label itself. Accepting the term *disabled* and using it politically against the dominant society, as the disability rights movement has sought to do,[5] was not a powerful enough strategy for Deaf people who sought to reject the pathological image. For Deaf people, the need for shared communication is far more pervasive than the need for participation in the public sphere. The strategies of the Deaf social movement, thus, attend to the need to preserve community, which will enable the continuation of shared communication.

Conclusion

The era of the 1960s and 1970s offered a new context for the Deaf social movement. While in the past Deaf people had struggled without much success to retain their sign language in the classroom, the attention given to the other movements rubbed off on the Deaf community. As a result, sign language was eventually transplanted back into the classroom. However, the distinctive modality of sign language presented a unique rhetorical challenge to the Deaf community, in contrast to the other liberating movements that shared the commonality of spoken languages with the dominant culture. The distinction of sign language inadvertently put it in a position of compromise, the route taken by the Deaf social movement.

The strategy of compromise, in the form of total communication, was an important step forward in the empowerment of the Deaf community. To jump from one extreme—oralism—to the other—sign language—would prove a difficult feat, given the near universality of speech and the determination of dominant discourses to retain spoken discourses. The Deaf social movement, therefore, chose the effective strategy of compromise.

Even as total communication appeased integrationists and even allowed them to glean their own interpretations of the philosophy, the Deaf movement benefited when total communication opened new avenues to them. For instance, research intensified, placing their sign language as an authentic language structure. Eventually, the Deaf movement was able to begin the slow but gradual shift from a compromise position to a more strengthened Deaf identity. The Deaf identity was validated with the establishment of the bilingual and bicultural identity.

The constitution of the Deaf community as a linguistic and cultural entity served also to depathologize the prevailing perception of Deaf people as "broken ears." The pathological depiction had paved the way toward social-engineering practices manifested by mainstreaming laws and the categorization of Deaf people as disabled. Rhetorical strategies, such as the self-defined bilingual and bicultural identity of Deaf people, sought to challenge these depictions. To further the defiance against pathological practices, mainstreaming was targeted as a symbol of the destruction of their community. The struggle by the Deaf social movement to spurn the practice of mainstreaming for all Deaf children also empowered, in that it led to other strategies.

These strategies—the creation of new discourse and artistic expressions in those discourses—opened newly established channels for the legitimacy of the language and culture of Deaf people. The legitimacy conferred upon their language—American Sign Language—embodied this newer movement. This was in contrast to an earlier era in which their sign language was not only not considered a language, but a modality not worthy of respect.

Even as integrationists continued to dominate educational and social service establishments and practices for Deaf people, the separatist rhetoric of the liberating movements influenced the newer shifts that marked the changes in the Deaf community. Separatist rhetoric enabled the Deaf community to bring sign language to a more respectable height. Further, it also brought on a stronger consciousness among Deaf people about their self-identity. Each strategy built on another and continues to stimulate the Deaf community to create further social changes. This would soon become evident with the advent of the Gallaudet University protest.

Notes

1. It should be noted that the term *language* is used here in its most generic sense. A language is a rule-governed system with a complex phonology, morphology, syntax, and discourse structure. There are also variants of languages, such as "dialects." A dialect is a regional variation of the dominant language and is distinguished by its "unique features of pronunciation, vocabulary, and grammar" (Dodd 1987, 140).

2. Arensberg and Niehoff explain the need to distinguish spoken (or signed) languages from written languages when differentiating one culture from another (1964). They argue that the distinction of a dominant language comes from its spoken (or signed) language, rather than its written language. For instance, England, the United States, and Ireland all use a similar form of written English, but they respectively speak British, American, and "brogue," or Gaelic.

3. Genovese argues that this form of resistance could not translate into collective action because this behavior traps the oppressed into a struggle with their oppressors instead of concentrating on developing a bonding with each other that could lead to liberation. I do not agree with Genovese's premise. It is necessary to "practice" resistance individually, before people can begin to resist collectively. In addition, the move to collective action cannot occur if the people within the oppressive situation do not feel oppressed. The reminder of these resistances can, in fact, serve as excellent examples of being oppressed. Thus, the experience of "resistance within accommodation," in addition to being a saving grace at the time of oppression, can also be a necessary prelude to some triggering event that creates collective action.

4. Argots differ from "foreign" languages in two major ways. The first difference is the association between sounds and meanings (Samovar and Porter 1991). In foreign languages, sounds differ, but meanings remain the same; for

example, the English sound for a greeting is "hello," while in Spanish, it is "hola." They both sound different but mean the same thing. With argots, the sound remains the same, but the meanings differ; for example, the African American dialect uses the term *bad* to refer to something very good, while in standard English the term means the opposite. While it is true that Black English differs from standard English in the referential meanings of certain vocabulary, this is not the only unique feature of Black English. Smitherman (1989) adds stylistic features "such as cadence, rhythm, resonance, gestures," and similar elements as a unique language pattern of Black English (Smitherman 1989, 296).

The second difference between argots and foreign languages has to do with cultural affiliations (Samovar and Porter 1991). With many foreign languages, for instance, one can determine the specific country by the name of the language. German denotes the country of Germany; French is spoken in France, and so on. Argots, on the other hand, do not refer to a dominant culture, but rather to specific groups within a dominant culture.

5. Joseph Shapiro, in a study of "disability" terminology, notes that many disabled people prefer terms such as "crippled," because it is a strategy to take "the most obvious, most scorned aspect of identity [which] was [then] transformed into a point of militant self-pride" (Shapiro 1991, C4; Shapiro 1994).

5

The Deaf President Now Protest

The era of the 1960s and 1970s saw the Deaf social movement move toward constituting the Deaf community as a linguistic and cultural group with a distinct identity. The separatist rhetoric that marked the changing consciousness of the Deaf social movement during that period paved the way to a strengthened "can do" rhetoric. Accordingly, the Deaf social movement began to align its new consciousness with demands for increased participation in the social and educational institutions that were involved with the Deaf community.

The 1987 resignation of Jerry C. Lee, then president of Gallaudet University, presented an opportunity to communicate such demands. The Deaf community had expressed the desire for a Deaf president at the time of the previous few vacancies but without success. Thus, when Lee and the previous president completed brief administrative terms, the Deaf movement once again began the call. This time, however, a rhetorical moment had presented itself. It was a time of uncertainty, with upheavals tied to administrative turnovers. Further, the Deaf community was strengthened by its sense of being a distinct cultural entity, which produced a more assertive rhetoric of their abilities.

However, the circumstances that greeted the Deaf movement at Gallaudet presented a shift in rhetorical context. For instance, how would dominant discourses that had prevailed at Gallaudet react to this new consciousness of Deaf people? Institutions such as Gallaudet constituted a paradox for the movement: it was a site primarily for Deaf people but most often run by hearing people. Prior to the Gallaudet uprising, there were a very small number of Deaf superintendents running residential schools for the deaf, and Gallaudet had never had a Deaf president. Consequently, as Deaf people began to assert "Deaf as good" and spurn the "Deaf as broken ears" image, this new sense of Deaf pride and "can do" rhetoric served to challenge the dominant hierarchy that placed hearing people in charge of their destinies.

When in March 1988 the Gallaudet board of trustees once again hired a hearing administrator during an era of increasing resistance toward the pathologizing of Deaf people, the Deaf President Now (DPN) uprising occurred. In the few weeks prior to the protest, Deaf leaders began organizing to build up the momentum for the call for a Deaf president. Letters, calls, and telegrams had been sent to the board of trustees and congressional leaders. A rally was held to build up and strengthen support for the cause. The rhetorical moment for a "Deaf President Now" was set in motion.

By the time the board of trustees made its announcement, expectations were very high. After all, of the three finalists, two were Deaf. However, the board of trustees announced their selection of Elisabeth Ann Zinser, vice chancellor of the University of North Carolina at Greensboro, yet another hearing person. Students shut down the campus for a week. Four demands were established: the resignation of Elisabeth Zinser, and her replacement with a Deaf president; the resignation of Jane Bassett Spilman, chair of the board of trustees; a restructuring of the board of trustees to create a 51 percent majority (at that time, only four of its twenty-one members were Deaf); and no reprisals against the protesters. By the end of the week, the board of trustees had agreed to meet all four demands. In addition, Philip Bravin, a Deaf board member, replaced Spilman and became the first Deaf chair of the board.

Where the choice of a hearing president at Gallaudet confirmed the prevailing pathological and paternalistic image of Deaf people, the demand for a Deaf president by the Deaf community challenged this perception. A Deaf president came to symbolize the rejection of the predominant pathological and paternalistic status of Deaf people.

The Symbolic Force of Paternalism

Dominant discourses of paternalism have always confined the Deaf community. Such rhetoric goes back to early Hebrew law: "If one exposes his cattle to the sun, or he places them in the custody of a deaf-mute, of a fool, or a minor, and they break away and do damage, he is liable" (Bender 1970, 19). The rhetoric of paternalism was also evident at the 1880 Milan Congress, when dominant discourses determined that the society at large was responsible for the care of Deaf people, perpetuating the myth that Deaf people could not determine their own fates. So what marked the difference this time around, in which the Gallaudet protest symbolized a refusal to condone further paternalistic discourses?

To understand the significance of the question, an examination of the rhetoric of the Gallaudet board of trustees and administration will reveal the prevailing ideology of paternalism. Additionally, it will be necessary to understand the impact of such an ideology on a marginalized group. So pervasive are dominant discourses of paternalism that they render a social movement immobile at times. Social movements then seek to transform into anger the internalized dominant discourses that serve as the wellspring of liberation. The question then arises: How did the Deaf social movement use this anger to mobilize the community for the Deaf President Now movement?

The Reign of the Plantation Mentality

Throughout the Gallaudet protest, the overriding rhetoric of the protesters indicated that Gallaudet was in some ways comparable to a plantation. The actual adoption of the plantation metaphor by the movement as a strategy, however, did not occur until the third day of the protest, when a Deaf faculty member declared:

"The time has come for the plantation mentality, which has for so long controlled this institution . . . to end" (Sinclair and Pianin 1988, A11). This characterization of the administration was a direct response to the dominant rhetoric of paternalism.

Dominant discourses that had prevailed for so long at Gallaudet bore evidence of a rhetoric of paternalism. The symbolic reign over Deaf students as well as the Deaf community was depicted in a variety of strategies adopted by the board, one of which was the rhetoric of "responsibility." The rhetoric of responsibility is a form of paternalistic discourse that gives others the responsibility for taking care of Deaf people. This rhetoric trades on the pathological viewpoint of Deaf people: if they are not complete persons, then they obviously need help in taking care of themselves. So pervasive was the paternalistic discourse that practices such as the board not knowing sign language—the integral component of the very people they purported to serve—indicated that they did not think it was necessary, since they were only looking after the interests of Deaf people. This attitude characterized board members who did not feel the need to communicate with Deaf people to find out what they thought their best interests were. The rhetoric of responsibility manifests itself in the adoption of parental tones, rather than in listening to those affected by the decision.

The rhetoric of "ingratitude," or an expression of resentment regarding the ungratefulness of those one is trying to help, is another aspect of paternalistic discourse. Such a practice is built on the parental belief that "children never appreciate what parents sacrifice for them." Spilman, then chair of the Gallaudet board of trustees, demonstrated this attitude in a statement she made after the uprising at Gallaudet: "I felt extremely hurt that not one deaf person came forward to say: Criticize this woman for anything you wish, but she has not performed in the abysmal, insensitive, uncaring fashion that you describe" (Dozier 1988, 16). This paternalistic rhetoric trades on the perception that Deaf people are "children." These "children" are so "ungrateful" that they do not realize how much their "care-takers," such as Spilman, have sacrificed for them.

The discourse of paternalism transformed into an institutional practice creates a cycle of dependency. Consider, for example, the rhetorical power of the myth of financial dependence. Edward C. Merrill, Gallaudet's president from 1970 to 1982, exemplifies this attitude in his attempt to intervene in the cycle: "I am informed enough to know that there are a few members who do not favor a deaf president and who state that it is doubtful that a deaf executive could manage budgetary matters well or could represent the University well in Congressional Hearings. These arguments are entirely spurious. These persons are probably insecure around deaf persons, and this produces a mind set that makes them overly cautious" (Merrill 1988). As Merrill points out, the argument that a Deaf person would have difficulty managing budgetary matters provided a means for board members to articulate their view of the inferiority of those for whom they were responsible. To argue that Deaf people could not manage finances became a strategy to prevent Deaf people from taking administrative positions. For one thing, the argument symbolized a lack of trust, which in turn signified a paternalistic view of Deaf people. For another, the argument embodied the perception that all Deaf people are alike. The rhetoric of the board indicated that it was all right to assume that no Deaf person could handle budgetary matters, without regard to their respective credentials. Further, this argument stipulated that a knowledge of budgetary matters took precedence over the significance of a Deaf president's running an institution for Deaf people. This perception also assumed that American Sign Language and Deaf culture were easier to learn than budgetary skills.

The paternalistic cycle of dependency and the accompanying reluctance to trust Deaf people in positions of authority, including the position of president of a university for Deaf people, was so pervasive that daily decisions reflected its strength. An electrician who was hired to perform electrical work on House

One, the president's home, asked Joan Lee, wife of Gallaudet's sixth president, whether she would not also want him to install wiring for light signalers that Deaf people often use to alert them that someone is at the door or that the phone is ringing. The electrician explained that this would make House One accessible to Deaf guests and would also be useful in the event that a Deaf president were chosen. Mrs. Lee brushed this suggestion aside with a laugh. The electrician went ahead and set the wiring in place without her knowledge and eventually returned to officially activate its use, this time for a Deaf president (R. Burrhus, personal communication, June 4, 1991).

This incident is only one example of the tremendous barriers that the Deaf protesters faced. So extensive was this paternalistic rhetoric of dependency that not only did the wife of Gallaudet's previous president find it ludicrous to imagine a Deaf president, she also was not convinced of the need to equip the house to make it accessible for Deaf people. That the house of Gallaudet's top executive, located right on the campus of the university, did not welcome Deaf people was not only paternalistic, but was also a snub to all Deaf people.

The Deaf Community: Internalized Oppression

The paternalistic discourses that dominated at Gallaudet, as well as the Deaf community, were strengthened and validated when Deaf people adopted such perceptions of themselves. Deaf people, as victims of these dominant discourses, had internalized the convictions of their oppressors. Paulo Freire points to this quality as "self-depreciation" (Freire 1970, 49). Self-depreciation comes about when oppressors of marginalized groups routinely and constantly denigrate the oppressed's sense of self-worth. So extensive is this practice that in the end, members of marginalized groups come to believe in their own inadequacy. Another feature that the Deaf social movement had to contend with was the dominant strategy of "divide and rule" (137). This strategy prevents marginalized groups from uniting and thus keeps the dominant hierarchy in place. Since these were two primary factors for the fractionalization of the Deaf community, the Deaf social movement had to counter them in order to effectively present itself as a united front.

The rhetoric of "self-depreciation" within the Deaf community was an internalization of the rhetoric of dependency instituted by paternalistic discourses. This rhetoric was evident in the way that many Deaf people had internalized the discourse of the dominant society—that Deaf people "can't." This saying is widespread throughout the Deaf community—virtually any Deaf person can recount tales of being told "you can't" do this or that because "you are deaf." That the rhetoric of dependency becomes internalized in a form of self-depreciation is confirmed by Ronald Sutcliffe, a Deaf administrator, as he relates his own experience: "Our teacher asked us what we would like to be after leaving school. One pupil wanted to be a truck driver. Another wanted to be a school principal. The teacher responded, 'Oh, you cannot be this because you are Deaf. You cannot be that because you cannot use the telephone.' We took it seriously. We were dependent on hearing people's judgments and opinions" (Schein 1989, 146). In the form of a self-fulfilling prophecy, many Deaf people internalized these dominant themes. Historical trends indicate that proportionally greater numbers of Deaf employees can be found in blue-collar and manual labor jobs than in white-collar jobs, and earn lower incomes in comparison to the general population (Rittenhouse, Johnson, Overton, Freeman, and Jaussi 1991; Schein 1989; Welsh 1991).

Particularly vulnerable to the rhetoric of "self-depreciation" were Deaf children of hearing parents. Most Deaf people came from hearing families, and hence were at risk of "double oppression." Unlike other marginalized people who can resort to the home as the sanctuary from the oppressive world, many Deaf people did not have this same refuge. The risk was tripled if they were "mainstreamed" into public schools, where they were unlikely to be able to seek comfort and support from Deaf peers either. Solomon explains that oppression can be extremely severe when it is applied to both the family and community systems

(1976). Consequently, these Deaf children were most at risk in facing extensive oppression, since they were likely to be surrounded by discourses that depreciated the positive Deaf identity.

This would indicate that many Deaf people were vulnerable to the internalization of disparaging discourses regarding their community. The power of the dominant society resides in its ability to influence the rhetoric of the masses under its control. Those who occupy positions of power—the dominant society—often claim the right to knowledge and discourse (Foucault 1980). Dominant discourses and practices are then accepted by most people without question. Thus, the paternalistic discourses that continued to prevail at Gallaudet strengthened and reinforced the internalization of their practices on those people being controlled. The acceptance of these paternalistic discourses then transforms into a rhetoric of "pathological limitation" as evidenced in the Deaf community.

The other challenge came in the form of "divide and rule" strategies or "dividing practices." Mainstreaming Deaf children was a practice that served to separate Deaf people from one another. These dividing practices contributed to differing viewpoints of the "Deaf identity" as a positive feature among Deaf people. Deaf people who internalized negative evaluations of the Deaf community, especially those who had minimal contact with other Deaf people or sign language, tended to have difficulty accepting or being accepted by the Deaf community. Virginia Covington explains the nature of the dilemma faced by these Deaf people as follows:

> They may never quite acquire competence in either [deaf or hearing cultures] but remain marginal. Superficially, they may look and act like hearing persons, without the facial expression play and expressive body movements that subtly distinguish the deaf. Their language and cultural attitudes also remain "hearing." Trained from infancy to prize speech and "proper English" of hearing persons, they may recoil from learning the sign language that will publicly identify them as deaf. Moreover, they fear that using sign language might lead to the loss of their speech skills and to alienation from their families. (Covington 1980, 271)

Thus, the positive perception of the Deaf identity would most likely be adopted by Deaf people who frequently encountered the Deaf community and sign language. The development of the Deaf identity then differs, usually according to the upbringing of Deaf people. This sense of identity, among other things, would have a significant impact on how a Deaf person viewed the urgency of having a Deaf president at Gallaudet University.

Other divisions split the Deaf community. Deaf African Americans, in Washington, D.C., and many other locations, have for years maintained their own social clubs or sports teams even though similar clubs for Deaf people were available nearby. Most social clubs established by Deaf people are predominantly white. Detroit, Michigan, has for years, hosted separate clubs for "oral" and culturally Deaf people, even though both groups use sign language. Deaf college graduates are often perceived as "snobbish" by others. These are only several examples of the many splits in the Deaf community which can make it difficult to collaborate as one big group.

At Gallaudet, these practices were maintained as well. For instance, a course that explores the various causes of deafness and the functions of the ear has been required of all students for years. It was not until November 1996 that the Faculty Senate voted to adopt an equivalent requirement for courses in Deaf culture and American Sign Language (Coogan 1996, 1). A Deaf Studies department was not established until January 1994, only after a Deaf president was finally in place. That a premier institution primarily for Deaf people, at the time of the protest, required a course that attends to the pathological, rather than the cultural, aspects of Deaf people, sent the message that the Deaf cultural identity was not valued.

Further, this practice is divisive. Many Deaf students come to Gallaudet without knowing sign language or being encultured into the Deaf community.[1] As Jerel Barnhart discovered, there are no programs that address cultural differences between Deaf and hearing people. Consequently, these Deaf students enter Gallaudet only to find themselves involved in cultural conflicts with other Deaf students (Padden and Markowicz 1976; Barnhart 1991). This creates a situation in which "the subjects' anxieties about changing their familiar behavior to accommodate newer, more acceptable behavior must be understood as a reaction toward conflicts arising from two cultures in contact. This study points to the need to recognize the Deaf community as a separate cultural entity, particularly for those who wish to join it as new members" (Padden and Markowicz 1976, 411). The paternalistic discourses that dominated Gallaudet created a perception of Deaf people as pathological. Thus, no serious attention was given to the development of cultural programs. Consequently, the rhetoric of pathology sustains dividing practices and upholds the negative perception of the Deaf identity.

Deaf leaders, in seeking to mobilize the community for the protest, needed to resolve the rhetorical dilemma of the internalized "pathological limitations" prior to working on the board of trustees. Not presenting a united front would give the board incentive to ignore pleas for a Deaf president. A divided nondominant group makes it easier for the dominant to prevail. They can simply say: "Well, we obviously can't please everyone, so we will just make the decision that we believe is best." Therein lies the problem for many marginalized movements. If they cannot unite, the dominant group will claim the right to continued reign over them. A case in point is the rhetorical dilemma the Black Power movement faced in the 1960s when the nonviolent factions of the Civil Rights movement led by Martin Luther King, Jr., focused their rhetoric on the integration of African Americans into mainstream society. The Black Power movement perceived this rhetoric as co-optation. This difference in ideology posed a rhetorical dilemma for Civil Rights leaders and the movement because it could not present a united front to the dominant society. The rhetoric of integrationists was at odds with the rhetoric of the Black Power movement, which stressed that white people had no place in Black people's lives.

The Gallaudet Protest: A Rhetorical Clash

The Gallaudet protest succeeded where previous attempts did not. This could be attributed to the themes of the protest. Every Deaf person, black or white, oral or signing, college graduate or not, associated with the Deaf community or not, can identify with the "can't syndrome" or the "plantation mentality." Because these themes reminded Deaf people of the many years of oppression, they were able to unite readily, even if only temporarily.

The mobilization of a movement is no easy feat, however. The difficulty of bonding social movements for a common cause is compounded by the "illegitimate" status of social movements.[2] Herbert Simons suggests that social movements can become legitimate if they adopt a combination of coactive and confrontational strategies (1972). Coactive strategies accentuate similarities with legitimate authorities, reinforcing the idea that societal norms and values should be respected. By virtue of sharing a common bond with the authoritative institution, the movement confers a status of legitimacy upon itself.[3] Strategies of confrontation, on the other hand, stress the dissimilarities and strive to strip institutions of their legitimacy. Thus, by diminishing the status of institutions, the strategy of confrontation also elevates the position of the social movement.

As the most effective and prominent movement in Deaf history, the Gallaudet protest adopted both coactive and confrontational strategies. These strategies turned pathological internalizations into anger that served as fuel for mobilization, in a series of stages.

Initiating the Protest

In the fall of 1987, shortly after Jerry C. Lee announced his resignation, various Deaf organizations began planting seeds for the call for a Deaf president at Gallaudet University (Christiansen and Barnartt 1995). The President's Council on Deafness, a group of Deaf faculty and staff at Gallaudet, held a "town hall" meeting and potluck supper to begin informal discussions about a Deaf president at the university. They also sent a series of letters to the board of trustees to encourage the active solicitation of potential Deaf candidates. The National Association of the Deaf also called on its leadership to plan strategy. A special edition of the association's newsletter focusing on the issue of a Deaf president was published in October 1987. The Gallaudet University Alumni Association and the National Fraternal Society of the Deaf also played a role by sending letters to the board. To ensure that qualified Deaf people were not overlooked, all of these organizations sent lists of potential candidates.

The groundwork for another crucial aspect of the protest—the rally—was established by a small group of Gallaudet alumni (J. E. Tucker, personal communication, November 5, 1991). This group identified itself as the "Ducks," representing "a close knit family of birds" who would work as a "flock" to accomplish their mission (Christiansen and Barnartt 1995, 12). The Ducks—Steve Hlibok, Mike O'Donnell, Jeff Rosen, Paul Singleton, James Tucker, and Fred Weiner—immediately worked toward building a coalition, securing financial as well as technical support from Deaf leaders, including business owners David Birnbaum and John Yeh. That influential leaders were supporting the Deaf President Now campaign gave legitimacy to the planned rally and prompted the student leaders into action. However, getting the students to buy into the cause had not been an easy task. The rhetoric of "Deaf pride" eventually drew the students in: the rallying cry during the last few days prior to the rally was, "where is your deaf pride?" (Christiansen and Barnartt 1995, 24). Once converted, the student leaders—Greg Hlibok, Tim Rarus, Jerry Covell, and Bridgetta Bourne—set about to convince the student body of the significance of the cause.[4]

A significant factor that characterized this stage was the number of Deaf leaders who have Deaf parents. These Deaf leaders were more likely to perceive the Deaf identity as a positive valuation through their early ties to their family, as well as the Deaf community. Solomon suggests that members of marginalized groups may not be as affected by rhetorical devaluations of themselves if "family ties or strong, cohesive group relationships provide a cushion of protection against them" (Solomon 1976, 21). Consequently, Deaf children of Deaf families may not face as oppressive an environment as other Deaf children, and thus may be more likely to react strongly when oppressive situations do arise.

This appeared to be the case at the Gallaudet protest—all four of the student leaders and the overwhelming majority of the Deaf alumni who spearheaded the rally had Deaf families. That Deaf children of Deaf families had a leading role at the protest is significant. Foucault maintains that those who occupy the highest levels of power structures claim the right to discourse and knowledge (1980). Since Deaf children of Deaf families had head starts in the cultivation of the Deaf identity and came to represent the highest levels of the Deaf hierarchy, they claimed the right and were granted the privilege of discourse and knowledge. This was demonstrated during the Gallaudet protest, when most of the leaders granted the power to discourse were Deaf children of Deaf parents.

For Deaf children of Deaf parents, who are most likely to accompany a positive identity with a "can do" attitude, the selection of a hearing president to run a premier Deaf institution constituted an insult. Indeed, a frequent rallying cry in the Deaf community is to "can the can't syndrome."[5] However, Deaf children of Deaf parents are in the minority within the Deaf community. It was thus up to them to persuade the majority of the Deaf community that now was the time to "can the can't syndrome" in their demand for a Deaf president.

The Rally

On March 1, 1988, a rally was held on the Gallaudet campus to raise the consciousness of those in attendance and to create a solidifying base. By then, the momentum was building, as three finalists had been announced—Harvey Corson, superintendent of the Louisiana School for the Deaf; Irving King Jordan, dean of the college of arts and sciences at Gallaudet University; and Elisabeth Zinser, vice chancellor of the University of North Carolina at Greensboro—and two of the three were Deaf. The rally was seen by many as the turning point of the movement, as it featured many prominent Deaf speakers, including Gallaudet faculty and staff, a dean from Gallaudet, leaders of organizations for Deaf people, and a local lawyer.

The fact that all the speakers were Deaf was a strategy to legitimize the Deaf identity. It gave Deaf students and their supporters the opportunity to witness a number of important Deaf role models all at once, a coactive strategy to bolster self-esteem and increase the sense of "Deaf pride," thus legitimizing the cause. The featured presenters were also making the confrontational statement that although they represented the most successful Deaf people, it was not enough. These leaders were in essence inciting their Deaf audience to dare to dream of a better future, one in which they could take control of their own destinies. So important was the aspiration to "take control over our [Deaf people's] futures," (cited in Sinclair 1988a, B7) that at least one speaker exhorted his audience to take on the challenge. Jeff Rosen, a Deaf attorney, declared: "People died in the civil rights movement. They were jailed in protesting the Vietnam war. I stand here in 1988 asking, 'What do you believe in? What is your cause?'" (Sinclair 1988a, B2). Here was a successful Deaf lawyer who not only presented legitimacy to the rally, but who challenged his audience to react.

The choice of Deaf speakers at the rally confronted the dominating practices of over a hundred years. After all, the symbolism of a Deaf president for Gallaudet represented very different implications for the Deaf community and the dominant society. For the dominant society, a Deaf president at Gallaudet merely signified upward mobility for Deaf people. And for most of the board of trustees, choosing a president was a difficult task, but it was just that—a task. The movement leaders, on the other hand, captured the Deaf community's understanding of what a Deaf president at Gallaudet would symbolize—an end to the "plantation mentality."

The importance of putting an end to the plantation mentality was articulated in the rhetoric of Deaf leaders throughout the protest. As Gary Olsen, then executive director of the National Association of the Deaf, would later say, "It's a national issue that affects all deaf people of all walks of life" (Bruske 1988, A16). Jack Levesque, executive director of an organization serving Deaf people in California, would note that "no one can imagine the ramifications for education, rehabilitation, and social service programs for deaf people all over the world when an international institution like Gallaudet makes the statement, 'Deaf people are in control of their own destinies'" (Johnstone 1988, 27). A Deaf president would also have tremendous impact on how Deaf children perceive themselves; as Olsen later said on *Nightline,* "I don't want my deaf children to believe that their only salvation is to be a hearing person." Having Deaf speakers at the rally was then an important strategy to most eloquently and convincingly convey the significance of a Deaf president.

Another strategy adopted during the rally was to move the audience from the football field to other pivotal places on campus, including the front of House One, where the president and his or her family would reside. This strategy encouraged a symbolic attachment to the sites on campus. Gallaudet is one of the few places where Deaf people constitute a demographic majority. The moving from place to place served to remind the audience that the campus was theirs—it was their home—where their "family" resided. Further, Jeff Rosen, in front of House One, pointed out that the president's home did not possess any of the devices found in most Deaf people's residences, such as TTYs or light signalers. But most important, it did not have a Deaf person living in it (DeLorenzo 1988).

Further, this strategy demonstrated the visibility of supporters for the cause. The estimated crowd of 1,500 people in attendance was, according to university officials, "unprecedented in its size and scope" (Sinclair 1988a, B1). At the very least, the large attendance would serve to illustrate that a good number of people were paying attention to the cause. It would also send a message to the board that a serious coalition was gaining momentum. The visibility of a large crowd at the rally would also serve to persuade those still on the fence of the legitimacy of the support for a Deaf president at Gallaudet.

The rally was successful in inspiring many Deaf people who had attended and in stimulating further action, as well as recruiting those who had remained hesitant. For instance, prior to the rally quite a few Deaf people had expressed ambivalence or concern about whether the university was ready for a Deaf president. The internalized "can't syndrome" spoke in such doubts as: Would a Deaf president be able to grasp fiscal responsibilities? Some worried that if a Deaf president did poorly, then future opportunities for a Deaf president would be lost forever. These concerns prompted at least one student to argue that only "the best qualified should be chosen," and to plead that the student body should "let the Board decide who is best qualified and accept" their decision (Cometor 1988, 5). The strategy at the rally was to break internalized dominant convictions by responding with "The time is now!" If Deaf people waited, when would it ever happen? The rally successfully produced a number of converts. Amy Hartwick, a Gallaudet student, for instance, had remained uncertain about the choice of a Deaf president until the rally, when she "realized" that she felt "very strongly" about the need for a Deaf president (Piccolli 1988, B1). The rally was a crucial stage in inspiring the audience and instilling a renewed sense of "Deaf pride." As one student attempted to explain, "I cannot find words enough to express how much the rally . . . inspired me. . . . This was, for me, a great expression of deaf pride" (Beckwith 1988, 7).

After the rally, students gathered in bull sessions, picketed and camped out at the Edward Miner Gallaudet building (where the president's office was located) and at the front gate of the entrance to the campus, and sent a letter to Zinser, the sole hearing finalist, urging her to withdraw her candidacy (Multra 1988b). In addition, an unfounded rumor circulated around campus that Spilman had called rally participants "a bunch of fools" (DeLorenzo 1988, 1). This strategy helped provoke the students to portray Spilman as the "enemy" even before the protest was begun. The depiction of Spilman as a devil figure was only beginning to emerge at this point and would eventually become an instrumental strategy for characterizing her as the symbol of the more than one hundred years of oppression.

These strategies before the final selection was announced were very visible and also served to exert pressure on the board of trustees, which was meeting on campus. These strategies were very effective in mobilizing the impetus for the movement. As it turned out, these demonstrations were a necessary prelude to creating expectations, firing supporters up, and setting in motion a coalition that was ready to move if things did not turn out as expected. The expectation that the next president would indeed be Deaf was overwhelming. After all, the board had chosen two Deaf candidates among its three finalists, and could the board really ignore the visible and enthusiastic demonstrations of support for a Deaf president?

Paternalism at Work

Apparently, however, the board could ignore the students' concerns—the movement strategies did not influence its final decision. Either the majority of the board did not take the strategies of the movement seriously, or their inability to communicate with Deaf people gave them an inaccurate reading of the mood on campus.

To the board, the two Deaf candidates were only tokens to appease Deaf people. In effect, the board's intent was to send a message to Deaf people that they were almost ready, but not this time around, maybe next time. Catherine Ingold, then provost at Gallaudet, demonstrates this paternalistic rhetoric: "Politically, we had to have some deaf candidates going forward to the board. Nobody questioned that. Even if none of them was qualified, we were going to do that" (Dozier 1988, 18). Not only did the discourse of paternalism dictate a rhetoric of responsibility, Ingold's statement demonstrated a willingness to patronize the Deaf community. The rhetoric of "tokenism" then, illuminated a perception that Deaf people could not possibly be "qualified," but the practice of choosing a few Deaf candidates would suffice to appease the movement. Further, the Deaf community would not object if a Deaf president was not chosen; after all, such a person was not "qualified."

Indeed, paternalism was evident in many of the rhetorical statements the administration made. Spilman herself purportedly "wanted so desperately to have a deaf president" that she carried around with her two pads to categorize the "positive" and "negative," where she could "jot down all the reasons we had to have a deaf president and all the reasons I didn't see how on earth we could" (Dozier 1988, 11–12). The language used by Spilman seems to be a contradiction. If, as she says, she wanted a Deaf president so "desperately," her choice of terminology for the "positive" and "negative" lists are not comparable. The phrase "reasons we had to have a deaf president" is more neutral than the rather dramatic "I didn't see how on earth we could." In her choice of terminology Spilman may have been trying to show the general public how agonizing the decision had been for her. However, the latter phrase also reveals her ideological viewpoint of the capabilities of Deaf people.

In addition, her lists considered only the issue of "deafness," rather than the persons involved. For Deaf people, this would make sense, because "Deafness" is a central feature of identity. For Spilman, however, it is more illustrative of lumping Deaf people together as a "condition." Her rhetoric here delineates the discourse of paternalism in her expressed need to make a pro and con list for having a Deaf president. She made no mention of making a similar list for having a hearing president, and it is rather doubtful that such a list was made.

For Spilman, the choice of a Deaf versus a hearing president came down to fiscal expertise, a traditional manifestation of paternalism. During the aftermath of the protest, Spilman explained: "They want a very visible, viable role model, and they think it is the most important thing they can do. And yet, if your institution wobbles and waffles from lack of clear direction or runs into trouble economically. . . . then it makes no difference if the person is hearing or deaf, if they cannot perform the job" (Dozier 1988,

12). In expressing this perception, Spilman's rhetoric is both con-descending and demonstrative of how out of touch she was with the pulse of the Gallaudet movement. Of course, she carefully included both hearing and Deaf candidates in her warning that an unqualified person could cause an institution to "wobble and waffle." However, the aspiration to which she is responding frames the implication that a Deaf university president would not be able to provide direction or fiscal management.

The strategies of the rally, while successfully inspiring the Deaf community to mobilize for the cause of a Deaf president, did not have the same impact on the board of trustees. The board of trust-ees maintained the stance that had served them well over the years. From the viewpoint of the board, "deafness" was not a criterion. Rather, the continued well-being of the university could occur only with a well-qualified person at the helm. However, the ques-tion of "qualification" created for the board a position disparate from that of the protesters. To the board, "deafness" was a condi-tion, and thus, a liability. Given that perception on the part of the board, the rally rhetoric was not persuasive.

Even though the rhetoric of the rally did not move the majority of the board, it may have been an instrumental factor in driving a wedge into the board that would eventually prevail. Philip Bravin, a Deaf member of the board, would later reflect: "I had worked hard to make people more aware of the needs of the deaf, that there needed to be a deaf president now, but apparently all the work did not carry enough weight. The hearing people were not ready or were not aware of the importance of having a deaf president" (Dozier 1988, 13). Bravin's statement reveals a break in the discourse of dominance on the board. A rhetoric of pater-nalism unites the board in carrying out its message of responsibil-ity to the community. Such rhetoric contrasts "responsibility" with "identity." The paternalistic discourse that had so prevailed on the board embodied the notion that "we have the responsibil-ity to make decisions for them." Bravin's statement highlights divisive rhetoric in the separation of the hearing and Deaf board members. Such a division confronts the previous unity of pater-nalistic discourses. It is a statement of the assertion of identity.

The Protest Begins

The Gallaudet protest was in essence a message that a new discourse would replace the discourse of paternalism. However, the success of the protest at Gallaudet was likely enhanced by the rally, which had served to unite and activate the Deaf community. As it was, Deaf people who flocked to the field house on that fateful evening of March 6, 1988, were expecting to celebrate the naming of their first Deaf president. They arrived to find that the board had not even extended the courtesy of a public announcement but had simply left a pile of news releases announcing the choice of Elisabeth Ann Zinser, the hearing candidate.

The numbing shock and disbelief at the continued paternalism of the board quickly turned into anger. That the board could so completely disregard their visible expressions of support for a Deaf president symbolized the continuing reign of the plantation owners. The intense reaction to this single instance of paternalistic communication came to articulate the years of repressed feelings about the continued attempts of the dominant society to control Deaf people.

The protest leaders moved to turn this frustration into support. As Bourne, one of the student leaders, would later define this moment: "We want to be free from hearing oppression" (Sanchez 1988, A12). The leaders declared an end to the time of compromise. It was now their call. They burned the news releases and, thereafter, did not recognize Zinser as their president. Zinser was called a "nonperson" and "not our president" by the students. So great was their anger that they immediately marched to the Mayflower Hotel, where the board was meeting.

There was no turning back now. A rhetorical moment had come, and the movement seized it. The students, as well as alumni, faculty, and staff, all started warming up outside of the hotel with chants of "Deaf President Now" and demands that the board come out. Deaf people were not there as good "children" to hear the board's explanation as to why a hearing person had been chosen. Rather, they wanted to confront the board, to confront paternalism. This became evident when after a long wait, Spilman and Phil Bravin, a Deaf board member, finally emerged.

The movement seized on confrontational strategies to portray Spilman as the "villain." Spilman had come out from the hotel flanked by one interpreter on each side and with Bravin barely visible behind her. This scene worked against Spilman in several ways. The arrangement of two interpreters, both signing at the same time, was not customary, especially with smaller crowds where one interpreter is clearly visible. This underscored Spilman's inability to communicate directly with the protesters. That two interpreters were needed also implied that Deaf people were so rowdy and difficult to communicate with that Spilman not only needed "bodyguards," but needed two people to help get the message across.

In addition, the portrayal of three hearing people (Spilman and the two interpreters) in the front and a Deaf person in the back (Bravin) implicitly sent the message that Deaf people were once again relegated to the back seat. The protesters reacted to this symbolic paternalism by refusing to listen to Spilman's explanations, shouting and booing at every turn. The group that remained at the hotel after a majority had left for a march to the White House then confronted Spilman, challenging her expertise by questioning her ability to use sign language. This strategy served to undermine Spilman's authority.

Although Bravin was termed a "Judas" and received many obscene calls during the week (Gannon 1989), the crowd that remained at the hotel that first night saw a different side of the story. His presence smacked of tokenism, but when the crowd demanded to hear from Bravin, he stepped forward and the group listened. What he had to say further supported their cause, for he explained that although there had been support for a Deaf president, the "majority had prevailed." Since the board was comprised of a hearing majority, Bravin's message was that qualifications were once again based on the dominant society's standards. Bravin had revealed a split in the board. No longer was the board simply undertaking the task of being "responsible" for the community, it was now apparent that the blanket of oppression extended to the Deaf members of the board as well. Bravin's statement of the "facts" exemplified the "can't syndrome," and redeemed him to the Deaf crowd at the hotel.

In a confrontation with several protesters the same night, Spilman purportedly made the infamous comment "Deaf people are not ready to function in a hearing world" (Pianin and Sinclair 1988, A21). Although she later claimed to have been misunderstood in her use of a double negative, purportedly having said, "Deaf people are not, not ready to function in a hearing world" (A21), this statement was widely quoted by the students and the media, which helped to portray Spilman as the villain.

The protesters had an "unexpected gift" in Spilman. It was easy to establish her as the ultimate villain, as she was a visible object who kept making statements that played right into the protesters' hands. Her rhetoric served to prove the students' charge of the plantation mentality. On March 7, 1988, the first day of the campus shutdown, when students blocked all the entrances and boycotted classes, Spilman was ushered into the field house to announce the board's position after a morning meeting to reconsider the demand for a Deaf president.

Apparently undeterred by the growing insistence of Deaf people with regard to their self-determination, Spilman stepped onto the stage to announce that the board's decision remained unchanged. Before she could proceed, however, Harvey Goodstein, a faculty member, came onto the stage to inform the audience that the board had decided to pay no heed to the students' demands for a Deaf president and further instructed everyone to leave. Spilman, not knowing sign language, did not grasp the situation and did not know why suddenly all hell had broken loose. In addition to people's leaving, much noise was generated, including that of a fire alarm. Spilman complained, "We aren't going to hear you if you scream so loudly that we can't have a dialogue" (Sinclair 1988b, A12). The students retorted, "What noise?" and "If you signed, we could hear you" (A12).

In a strategy of confrontation, where Spilman's inability to use sign language was exploited, the protesters seized upon the moment to assert the authority of their mode—sign language. The symbolism of the noise also demonstrated that contrary to popular views of Deaf people as "silent," the students were not silent. Further, they were very aware of sound and used it to their advantage. Extreme noise is not as bothersome to Deaf people as it is to hearing people. Recognizing this, the protesters blatantly generated as much noise as they could to thumb their noses at authority, doing so in as annoying a way as they could.

Confrontational strategies such as these are often used by movements because of their potential to expose the real positions of the opposition. In response to provocation, members of the dominant opposition may be caught off guard and say things that reveal their true beliefs. Spilman dug a hole for herself when she made such incriminating statements, and when authorities lose control in this fashion, their legitimacy is challenged. Since the showdowns at the protest were successful in exposing Spilman's true ideology, the media picked up on it and assisted the protesters in portraying Spilman as the antagonist.

The Escalating Forces at Battle

With the assistance of the media, the Gallaudet protest was for the most part characterized favorably. This unexpected support from the media could be attributed to a number of factors. One was that the protesters were more accessible to the media, as the board members and Gallaudet administration were for the most part unavailable (Christiansen and Barnartt 1995). The location of Gallaudet University in the nation's capital, where civil rights marches (the movement that DPN was most compared to) took place, also played on the symbolism of democracy. This was also the home of the *Washington Post,* which covered the protest extensively. The *Post*'s national visibility increased the likelihood that the media elsewhere would pick up the story and emulate the positive coverage given by the *Post* (Christiansen and Barnartt 1995). Compassion for the students was another factor. One reporter explained the fascination with the story, "This little kid

[Greg Hlibok] going up against the big guys, playing hardball with the administration and winning" (Christiansen and Barnartt 1995, 188). It was also true that the media and other outside groups had nothing to lose in their support for the protest. They could thus easily endorse the rationale that the protesters should get what they want, because what they wanted was to have one of their own as their leader.

This support from the media and other outside groups allowed the movement to gain momentum as support continued to increase. The Gallaudet University Alumni Association voted its support of the protest, and its president flew in from California to participate in the events. The Gallaudet faculty also voted 147 to 5 to endorse the demands. Moe Biller, the American Postal Workers Union president, and Mitch Snyder, an advocate for the homeless, came on campus to lend their support. Money flowed in. Students at the California (Fremont), Georgia, Illinois, Maryland, Missouri, and Rhode Island schools for the Deaf held rallies (Gannon 1989). Students at the Southwest Collegiate Institute for the Deaf in Big Spring, Texas, marched through the city (Gannon 1989).

As movements garner support for their cause, the opposition builds up resistance. This occurred for the Gallaudet protest on Wednesday, March 9, when Zinser abruptly left her post in North Carolina and came to Washington. After consultations with a public relations firm about strategies to resolve the growing issue, Spilman had asked Zinser to come to Washington, D.C., to be closer to the situation and to help maintain control. At an ensuing press conference on the same day, two strategies by the opposition further irked the protesters. Zinser evidently miscalculated the intensity of the protest and declared, "I am in charge" (Pianin and Sinclair 1988, A20). She asserted her authority to exert control over what she perceived to be several leaders trying to usurp the power of the trustees. This strategy backfired, however, because by this time, it was not only the students who were actively participating, but many other Deaf adults as well. Her attempt to take over the campus also exemplified the parental tone that dictated a "take charge" attitude toward "disruptive children"—the very discourse of paternalism that the protesters were exploiting.

The board's press briefing also backfired when it furthered the perception of the Gallaudet administration as the villains. The board's strategy was to claim that the two Deaf finalists supported the decision to appoint Zinser. However, the appearance of a pallid-looking I. King Jordan at the briefing did not appease the protesters as hoped. Rather, they turned his appearance into fuel for further speculation among the protesters of their power. Faculty members at a special meeting pointed out that Jordan's "appearance and manner would have led one to question whether he was truly speaking his mind" (Faculty minutes 1988, 1). A call to Harvey Corson, the other Deaf candidate, also confirmed that he had not avowed his support for Zinser ("Corson Denies" 1988).[6] It was further reported that "several administrators are being coerced into refraining from supporting the strike" (Faculty minutes 1988, 1). These accounts, suggesting that the administration was now using the force of intimidation on Jordan as well as on other top-level Deaf administrators, spread and infuriated many. Consequently, these charges served to portray Spilman and her cronies as evil figures.

The strategy of "recruiting" support from Jordan and Corson worked against the administration in more dramatic ways. Jordan was first portrayed as a victim, then a hero. The protesters were rewarded for standing their ground when Jordan retracted his support for Zinser the next day. In doing so, Jordan rhetorically created a bond with the protesters and legitimized their cause. He related his "personal reaction to the Board's decision" which was "anger at the continuing lack of confidence in . . . deaf people" (Jordan 1988, press release). Jordan now symbolized the struggle of the movement. No longer was the rhetoric of the decision centered around a question of "qualifications," it became a condemnation of paternalistic discourses. Consequently, his support and expressed anger presented legitimacy to the protest and propelled him into the role of the hero.

After all, only a Deaf person could fully empathize with the cause of the movement. As Jordan later indicated, he chose to support the protesters rather than the administration, because: "My role as dean or president of Gallaudet is temporary. My deafness is not" (Dozier 1988, 12). Jordan's statement rejected the pathological view of deafness that so predominantly framed the perception of the board. Further, it declared his affiliation with the movement and its struggle for self-identity. Jordan knew his community. He knew he could not abandon Deaf people, but most of all he could not abandon his "Deaf" self.

Two other rhetorical moments considerably weakened the board's position. The first occurred on *Nightline* on Wednesday evening, on which Hlibok, Deaf actress Marlee Matlin, and Zinser were featured guests. Zinser invoked the wrath of both Hlibok and Matlin with her statement: "I believe very strongly that a deaf individual [will] one day . . . be the president of Gallaudet." Deaf people had heard it all before and were very tired of it. Both Hlibok and Matlin interrupted Zinser, an emotional Matlin saying, "Why not now? Why not now?" Hlibok brushed Zinser off, saying, "That's old news. I'm tired of that . . . one day, again and again, someday a deaf person. We've got to break this cycle. The past presidents have always said that. Some day." Ted Koppel then lent his support to the protesters by questioning Zinser's authority, "If you'll forgive my saying so, Dr. Zinser, it's a little bit disingenuous to suggest that you are some kind of puppet who cannot act on her own because the board has said, 'You're in.'"

The other was to bring the protest to the attention of the United States Congress. Congressional members David Bonior and Steve Gunderson, Gallaudet board trustees who had not attended the meeting to vote for Zinser, were instrumental contacts for the protesters. On Thursday, March 10, they solidified the protesters' position by questioning the validity of the board's stand and contending that the students' demands—Zinser's resignation and replacement by a Deaf president; Spilman's resignation; a restructuring of the board of trustees to create a 51 percent majority; and no reprisals against the protesters—were reasonable. Bonior even suggested that it might be in everyone's best interests for Zinser to resign. This congressional support helped destroy the myth created by the board that a Deaf president could not readily handle funding requests from Congress. Since the bulk (75 percent) of Gallaudet's financing came from Congress, the board's justification that Zinser would help maintain that funding no longer held water.

The cause of the Gallaudet protest was notably legitimized by the media and members of the dominant society in these and other instances. Although the media are made up of members of the dominant society, they were able to empathize with the Deaf protesters. This suggested the existence of a symbiotic relationship between two entirely different segments of American culture. Such a message was that if the predominantly hearing Congress and media could understand and endorse the rationale for the protest, then the conflict was between the protesters and the paternalistic plantation owners, rather than between Deaf and hearing people.

A Journey through the Rhetoric of Mockery

Ted Koppel's depiction of Zinser as a "puppet" was quickly transformed into a symbol of paternalism and stimulated a flurry of rhetorical strategies centered around the theme. As the momentum of the movement stepped up, so did the intensity of collective mockery. That the puppet theme particularly rejuvenated the protesters had historical implications. It symbolized years of ongoing resistance to domination by educators, administrators, and other representatives of the "human sciences." The imposition on Deaf people of speech training and other "normalizing" strategies, as well as the "can't syndrome," were equivalent to controlling Deaf people. As such, Deaf people were treated as "puppets." Now, by taunting Zinser as a "puppet," they were emancipated. They were able to retaliate by shedding their "puppet" image and presenting it to a nemesis who epitomized the many years of paternalism.

The rhetoric of mockery, including the illustrative puppet

This poster from the Deaf President Now protest plays on the puppet theme.

theme, provided the students with a legitimate opportunity to assail Spilman and Zinser. A collective form of mockery allowed the protesters to demean their opponents' credibility while strengthening their own. This strategy was accomplished by mocking Spilman and Zinser as well as burning their effigies on the football field. This form of ridicule is constructive in that it allows the protesters to reject the social order and institute a new order. Kenneth Burke calls this process the "symbolic kill" as a reference to the "desire to transform the principle which that person represents" (Burke [1945] 1969, 13). For Burke, the symbolic kill "is a special case of transformation" in which "the killing of something is the changing of it" (19–20).

For Deaf people, the mockery of Spilman and Zinser signified a symbolic kill in which the oppressors and the principles they represented were "killed." By killing the representatives of their oppression, Deaf people set themselves free. Spilman and Zinser symbolized the "plantation mentality" so often quoted during the week. That Deaf people killed the image of themselves as slaves or puppets and transformed themselves into the "regime" was evident in the themes of many of the posters.

One poster showed Deaf people first as puppets, with ropes secured around the mouth, symbolizing the imposition of oralism, and then emancipated, free of the ropes and handcuffs. The slogan on it was "The 'CAN'T SYNDROME' is NO MORE!" Another poster portrayed the earth as "DEAF WORLD" and both Spilman and Zinser squashed underneath. Yet another poster featured Spilman losing control while the enraged Bison (Gallaudet's mascot), wearing severed shackles, brandished a pair of scissors cutting off Spilman's "puppet" hold on Zinser. Zinser is shown falling while a book she has been trying to learn ASL from falls out of her hands.

These posters demonstrated the killing of the old image of Deaf people as slaves under the control of slave masters on a plantation for a new one of Deaf people in control of a new world. This new world was theirs, and in this new order, Deaf people and their language would not be demeaned. That Spilman thought it unnecessary to learn sign language or that Zinser believed she could learn ASL and Deaf culture from books in a matter of weeks would be events that could occur only in the old order. This new society allowed the Alice Cogswell of old to grow up. No longer would Alice be content to merely lean against Thomas Gallaudet, gazing adoringly up at him. She was now a liberated Deaf person, fully in charge of her destiny.[7]

Mockery as a rhetorical tool to create a bond among Deaf people and their supporters against the dominant order became a popular strategy, especially during the later stages of the protest. Signed chants of "Spill-man" and "Sinner" maintained the inspirational tone of "us against them." An ASL lesson for Spilman

(*Above*) This poster from the Deaf President Now protest illustrates Deaf people's emancipation from oralism and oppression.

(*Left*) Jane Bassett Spilman and Elisabeth Zinser are overpowered by the "Deaf World" in this poster.

This series of illustrations depicts the transformation of Alice Cogswell from an adoring student into a liberated, independent person.

was "home-go-now." Jokes went around to the effect that Zinser now knows three signs, "Deaf-president-now." A saying went that "Dr. Zinser is not ready to function in the Deaf world." Even a dog was seen trotting around with a cloth: "I understand sign better than Spilman." These forms of ridicule served to intensify the gap between Deaf people and the two outsiders who embodied the oppression of everything Deaf people stood for.

By creating such a gap, the protesters could reveal the weaknesses of the oppressors and pave the way for a redistribution of power. That the rules were different for hearing and Deaf people did not go unnoticed by the protesters. Only by exposing the inequities of rules maintained by dominant discourses could a transformation occur. Christine Multra, in an editorial for the student newspaper, noted this double standard:

> Who cannot help but laugh ironically at Spilman's statement that Zinser "fit all the criteria with the exception . . . of understanding deafness and deaf culture?" Zinser says she is learning sign language

Shortly after Elisabeth Zinser announced her resignation, students created this poster proclaiming that they still had three-and-a-half demands left.

and reading books on deaf education and deaf culture. Bravo Zinser! Rules are different for hearing people, you see. They are allowed to remedy their deficiencies by reading, but deaf people are not allowed similar privileges [*sic*]. Consistency, truly thou art a jewel! (Multra 1988a, 5)

A New Order

Soon after the *Nightline* episode, on Friday morning, March 11, Elisabeth Zinser announced her resignation. At noon the same day, the protesters, in a festive mood, marched from Gallaudet to the Capitol, avowing that they still had "three and a half demands to go." Patterned after the civil rights movement, the four student leaders led the march with a banner reading, "We still have a dream." On Sunday, March 13, at a press conference, Philip Bravin announced that Spilman had resigned, that he was the new chair of the board, and that Irving King Jordan had been selected as Gallaudet's eighth president.

Deaf people could look back on their efforts at the Gallaudet protest with pride, for this was a hard-fought struggle they had won. Not only did they achieve all four demands, they also received a bonus in the form of Bravin, the newly selected board of trustees' first Deaf chairperson, for the protesters had called for a Deaf majority on the board, but not a Deaf chair. Most important, it taught Deaf people that they could wage an effective battle and win. The newly announced President Jordan said as much in his victory speech:

> In this week we can truly say that we, together and united, have overcome our own reluctance to stand for our rights and our full representation. The world has watched the deaf community come of age. We will no longer accept limits on what we can achieve. And I must give the highest of praise to the students of Gallaudet for showing us all exactly how even now one can seize an idea with such force of argument that it becomes a reality. (Gannon 1989, 144)

Indeed, for Deaf people, a victory meant the creation of a new image. A new vision for Deaf people and the world watching them was that indeed, Deaf people "can." To effectively realize this image, Deaf people had to "produce, reinvent and create the ideological and material tools they need[ed] to break through the myths and structures that prevent[ed] them from transforming an oppressive social reality" (Giroux 1983, 226). The strategies adopted by Deaf people throughout the protest effectively destroyed many of the negative images maintained by dominant discourses and substituted a newer image of the able competence of Deaf people.

Indeed, the success of a social movement and the ensuing transformation of the perception of the group has empowering capabilities. Not only does the dominant society begin to perceive the dominated group differently, but the dominated individuals increase their feelings of self-worth. Elsasser and John-Steiner note that a "sense of personal power and control emerges largely as a result of the increasing movement of his or her social group towards self-determination" (Elsasser and John-Steiner 1977, 356–57). The experience of success that comes with such a victory produces feelings of self-worth and control as well as an increased awareness of oppressive tendencies. It thus becomes more difficult thereafter to accept perceived injustices based on one's marginalized status. As student leader Bourne put it, "This is not the end; this is the beginning" ("Deaf Protesters," 1988, A1).

Conclusion

Previous collective action had resulted primarily in the preservation of self-respect for Deaf people. The Gallaudet protest, however, also gained respect from many members of the dominant society. In some cases, hearing people realized that previous perceptions of Deaf people based solely on their sense of hearing were not appropriate. As one letter writer noted, "I now see myself less as 'hearing-able' and more as 'signing-illiterate'" (Gannon 1989, 134).

The protest also signified a struggle for Deaf ownership. Implicit in the controversy was the struggle between integration and separatism. Some perceived the protest as an avowal of support for separatism. A minister with no apparent affiliation with the Deaf community wrote in a letter to the editor of the *Washington Post:* "It cannot become a chapel or a kingdom unto itself. It would lose contact with the surrounding world and become a foreign enclave. . . . True wisdom [is to] . . . have the head of Gallaudet be a person of the hearing community who would help lead graduates into the mainstream of American life, of which he or she is a vital part" (Stein-Schneider 1988, A24). In his dissertation about the protest, Mark DeLoach makes a similar argument. He contends that the move in the direction of separatism symbolized in the Gallaudet protest would not be a positive change in that it would continue to maintain the distance between the Deaf and hearing worlds (DeLoach 1990).

Deaf people, however, did not perceive the Gallaudet protest as a theme of separatism. Rather, many saw it as a step toward self-governance and, thus, pride and empowerment of their community. Jamie Lowy explains, in a letter published in the *Post* the same day as Stein-Schneider's letter, that she herself grew up in a mainstream environment and took "little pride in being deaf" (Lowy 1988, A24). Not until she entered colleges for Deaf people (NTID and later Gallaudet) did she begin "to really develop an identity as a deaf person. By the time I graduated, I was able to say 'I'm proud to be me, and I'm proud to be deaf'" (A24).

Thus, one of the primary empowering functions of the Gallaudet protest was to promote an environment that fostered a positive view of Deaf identity. Further, although the Gallaudet protest signified a form of separatism to some people, Deaf people perceived it differently. Since American society had not yet conformed to the needs of Deaf people, this form of separatism was bred out of necessity. And if Deaf people were going to be, in a sense, segregated from society, then they would be further empowered by having representatives of their own community governing them. The Gallaudet protest was, then, an empowering movement to enable Deaf people to further empower themselves.

Another strategy that contributed to the success of the Gallaudet protest was the choice of themes. Themes such as "can the can't syndrome" and the "plantation mentality" represented issues that likely struck at the heart of many, if not most, Deaf people. Such a strategy also empowers because it unites. The Deaf community had faced much difficulty in creating large-scale unity in the past in large part due to the inability to polarize divergent ideologies. The themes at the Gallaudet protest, however, crossed these divisions.

The strategies of legitimacy and confrontation also led to a strengthening of Deaf pride and empowerment. Legitimacy gives credibility to a movement, and without gaining respect from insiders and outsiders, a movement may be perceived as merely a fad or the work of crazed radicals. However, a movement cannot move on without confrontational rhetoric. A polarization of ideologies is needed to create change.

The Gallaudet protest established legitimacy through a number of strategies. The rally organizers strategically chose presenters who were all respectable, prominent Deaf leaders. The student

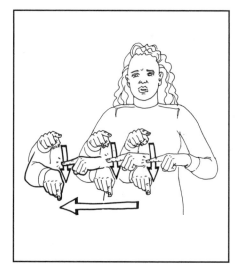 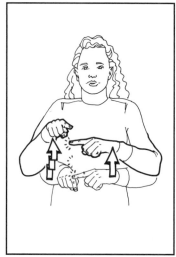

The sign on the left exemplifies the "can't" syndrome, while the sign on the right was created to symbolize the positive efforts of the "can the can't syndrome" movement. The repeated upward movement of the second sign provides a sharp contrast to the negative, downward movement of the first sign.

leaders were active in campus affairs and had the respect of the student body. Support was garnered from the faculty, who endorsed the protest. Various national organizations were also contacted to lend their support. After his initial hesitation, I. King Jordan declared his strong support for the cause, a decision he made after long discussions with his wife and former Gallaudet president Edward C. Merrill, who told him to "listen to your heart" (Christiansen and Barnartt 1995, 136). The organizers also established a significant relationship with the media and were rewarded by a stamp of approval that helped to promote the students' cause.

Confrontational rhetoric also empowers because it gives the protesters a sense of control. By giving voice to the rhetoric of "NO," the Gallaudet protesters challenged the authority of the administration. The rhetoric of confrontation used by the protesters also included the mockery of Spilman and Zinser as villains. This strategy empowers, because as Richard Gregg points out, "by painting the enemy in dark hued imagery of vice, corruption, evil, and weakness, one may more easily convince himself of his own superior virtue and thereby gain a symbolic victory of ego-enhancement" (Gregg 1971, 82).

Notes

1. There is a New Signers Program at Gallaudet that offers sign language instruction to incoming students who need it. However, the program lasts approximately three weeks, and students have commented that they needed more sign language instruction (Barnhart 1991).

2. Social movements appear illegitimate in contrast to the symbolic authority of institutions. Dominant practices so pervasively intimidate people into deferring to authorities, such as "legitimate" institutions (McGuire 1977), that: "violation[s against "legitimate" establishments, e.g., social movements] would be shunned in order to avoid the feelings of guilt or shame which would follow" (Kriesberg 1973, 111).

3. Robert Cathcart places the responsibility of legitimacy on the leadership, which "is not recognized, for it has no legitimacy, and to confer with it would be tantamount to doing business with the devil" (Cathcart 1978, 246). Rimlinger, on the other hand, suggests that the success of social movements requires that their modus operandi somehow become legitimate to institutions, the general public, and potential recruits to the movement (1970).

4. Only one of the student leaders immediately embraced the cause (J. E. Tucker, personal communication, November 5, 1991).

5. To embody the "can the can't syndrome," a sign was created: in lieu of signing "can," the sign "can't" is done in a fashion that transforms the negative implication into a positive one (see p. 134).

6. It was later explained that Harvey Corson had sent Zinser a letter of congratulations earlier in the week, before the protest escalated to the point when Zinser pointed to the letter as an endorsement (Christiansen and Barnartt 1995).

7. This is a reference to the young Deaf girl who became Thomas Gallaudet's first student. An earlier chapter describes how Gallaudet went on a mission to find the best means of educating Deaf students. Gallaudet, along with two other men, went on to establish the first school for the Deaf in the United States. The statue of Alice Cogswell leaning against Gallaudet and gazing up at him is a landmark at Gallaudet University (see p. 60).

6

Seeking a Diversified America

The Gallaudet protest phase of the Deaf social movement typified what Stewart, Smith, and Denton characterize as
the "enthusiastic mobilization" stage (1989, 25). During this
stage, optimism among movement participants climaxes. Social
movements, however, cannot remain in the enthusiastic mobilization stage for long periods of time because of the high level of
energy required to maintain this stage. Society, the media, and
even the participants become exhausted and turn their attention
elsewhere. Most movements enter the "maintenance" stage at this
point (28). The maintenance stage represents a crucial time, the
point when a movement determines its future direction. The Deaf
social movement has likewise entered the maintenance stage in
the period following the Gallaudet protest, as it determines its
contemporary strategies.

Although the contemporary Deaf social movement has not solidified to the point where it can be studied as a fully accomplished
rhetorical phenomenon, the strategies that mark this stage thus
far indicate an emerging rhetorical form. The Deaf social movement in the United States after the Gallaudet protest has capitalized on the move by African Americans, Native Americans,
Hispanic Americans, and others to create community through the
promotion of cultural diversity.

The rhetorical trends of these cultural diversity movements
exemplify three necessary attributes for community building
within a multicultural ideology: creating a sense of self-worth,
establishing an internal foundation for community building, and

137

participation in the public sphere. This newer ideology stipulates that these attributes promote the preservation of each culture, not only to enable marginalized peoples to take pride in their cultural identity, but also to foster greater multicultural tolerance and acceptance within the dominant society. Therefore, striving for a greater amount of ownership within a marginalized community corresponds to a greater demand for participation in public life and ultimately contributes to a more pluralistic society.

Balancing Integration and Separatism

The post-1960 multicultural movements balance separatism and assimilation. As Lisa Jones, daughter of African American poet Amiri Baraka, puts it, diversity movements seek "to fuse self-help and the fight against racism together into one" (Harrington 1991, 25). These movements have made inroads in creating Women's Studies and African American Studies at many universities and curricula that reflect the diversity of cultures in America. The cultural diversity movements have also been embraced by more members of the dominant society than was the case with, for instance, the Black Power movement.

The cultural diversity strategy has, however, adopted many of the goals of the earlier separatist movements, including such goals as creating a sense of pride in cultural groups and establishing the power to make decisions that affect the lives of members. For example, Black Power presented the 1960s with a growing militancy that threatened many members of the dominant society. Many integrationists, such as Roy Wilkins, the executive director of the National Association for the Advancement of Colored People (NAACP) in 1966, fearing a backlash of civil rights efforts, painted the dominant sentiment of Black Power as symbolic of "antiwhite power"—a hatred for white people and for America (cited in Handler 1966, 14). Since many people also believed Black Power proponents preached violence, it was feared that this "hatred" would become violence.

However, critics have noted the prevalent societal misinterpretations of the phrase. Scott and Brockriede explain that to people like Stokely Carmichael, Black Power symbolized "personal pride in being black, responsibility to other blacks, and power as a group to deal with outsiders" (Scott and Brockriede 1969, 5). Inherent in Black Power rhetoric was the struggle for the right of marginalized peoples to define and identify themselves (Scott and Brockriede 1969; Campbell 1971).

Scott and Brockriede also point out that contrary to rejecting involvement in the public sphere, Black Power was a statement in support of *institutionalized* integration rather than *individualized* integration; in other words, integration as promoted in civil rights legislation benefited only the most "qualified" African Americans rather than the entire group. Further, Campbell argues that the violence threatened in Black power was symbolic "because it threatens, because it is frightening, [it] assures him of his equality, dignity, and manhood. When so assured, it becomes possible for the Black man to confront the White man as an equal, with pride, self-respect, and dignity" (Campbell 1971, 159).

The cultural diversity strategy is an expanded descendant of the Black Power movement. However, rather than using the rhetoric of "power," which is seen as threatening by the dominant society, the movements adopt words such as "cultural diversity," and "multiculturalism." These terms succeed where Black Power struggled, since they play on the democratic idealism of America. Cultural diversity sends the message that America, the home of freedom and opportunity to numerous immigrants, would be mean-spirited to begrudge marginalized groups that same right, especially if her strength comes from that diversity. Where Black Power demands group integration, cultural diversity extends an invitation to society to celebrate along with marginalized groups their culture and identity as a solution to institutional integration. Further, Black Power speaks for African Americans, while cultural diversity presents a spirit of coalition for all dispossessed groups.

In effect, cultural diversity has transformed Black Power rhetoric into a position of respectability. Additionally, cultural diversity presents a solution to integrationists in the form of equal participation in the dominant society. By legitimizing the preservation of unique groups within the dominant society, cultural diversity becomes a strategy to ensure participation in public life.

The Deaf Movement Adopts the Multicultural Ideology

The rhetorical trends of the Deaf social movement since the Gallaudet protest indicate this direction as well. The Deaf social movement uses strategies developed by other social movements to find a balance between separatism and assimilation within a multicultural framework. Through these strategies the movement develops a sense of self-worth, builds a strengthened internal foundation of their community, and commands greater involvement in public life.

Creating a Sense of Self-Worth

One function of social movements is to develop a sense of self-worth among its members. At Gallaudet this was achieved through the many confrontations with the board. But in the post-Gallaudet atmosphere, the movement has sought to provide an ongoing rhetoric to establish self-worth in more pervasive ways that serve as a basis for acceptance of the Deaf community within a framework of diversity. Legitimizing the group identity as "the good" serves to instill pride and creates a buffer against dominant characterizations of the group as "the bad" or the "deviant." The sense of self-worth that emerges is a crucial element if social movements are to succeed in establishing communities within a dominant society.

The aftermath of the Gallaudet protest has produced within the Deaf social movement a new rhetoric of assertion that performs a sense of self-worth. Perhaps the comparison of an old and a more recent Deaf joke illustrates. The age-old joke takes variations of this form:

There was once a Deaf man who was driving until he came to some train tracks. However, he was not able to drive through because the crossing signal gates were blocking his way. After waiting for a very long time, the Deaf man got out of the car and walked to where the gate controller was stationed. While the gate controller was talking on the phone, the Deaf man wrote on a piece of paper, "please but." The gate controller couldn't figure out what the Deaf man was trying to get across.

This joke does not make sense to nonsigners because it is based on a sign play. The written word *but* is a reference to a sign in ASL that means "to open the gate," which is also the sign for the word *but*. The more recent joke takes this form:

A Deaf person was riding on a train and met a Cuban and a Russian. After smoking only half a cigar, it is thrown out the window. The Deaf person asks, "Why did you throw that out?" "Oh," says the Cuban, "we have plenty of cigars in Cuba." Later, the Russian throws out a half-empty bottle of vodka. "We have plenty of vodka in Russia," says the Russian. The Deaf person contemplates all this. Then, as a hearing man walks by, the Deaf person picks him up and throws him out the window. "We have plenty of hearing people in this world" is the explanation.

Douglas explains that jokes reveal the marginalized group's vision of the inequalities in society, and this one articulates a vision of a strong Deaf person challenging an inferior status (1968).

The "but" joke establishes the gatekeeper in the symbolic role of the hearing person who is frequently in control of the Deaf person's destiny and pokes fun at Deaf people's struggles with English. Anthropologist Susan Rutherford explains that this joke is "a picture of lack of control, lack of self-determination, negation of identity, stifled development, blocked communication, external control characterized by benevolent paternalism and authoritarianism" (1989, 76).

In contrast to the older joke, the newer joke demonstrates a sense of power and control, depicts self-determination, and is a positive enactment of the Deaf identity. However, hearing people often express distaste for this joke. Such a response is to be expected, because there is a rhetoric of confrontation—even a threat—in the joke. If expressive of a mood of many Deaf people in more recent times, it bodes a challenge. Nevertheless, the transformation of consciousness evident in the two jokes exemplifies the new sense of self-worth. The previous joke that mocks the Deaf person as the "deviant" reinforces societal perceptions. The newer joke rejects the negative depiction and symbolically substitutes "the bad" for "the good."

Oppressed groups often use humor as a coping strategy against prejudice and discrimination from the dominant culture. Humor enables an oppressed group to symbolically condemn its unequal status and to transform its "misery by poking fun at oppressors" (Fine 1983). By attacking the dominant culture, a symbolic release from oppression translates into the inculcation of pride, of self-worth in marginalized peoples, thus creating a strengthened framework for cultural diversity (Martineau 1972).

Another example of such humor, perhaps less pointed but still confrontational, appeared in the treatment of the hearing aid[1] in the comic strip "Oxford," created by Bruce Hanson, featuring a Deaf monkey. The Deaf monkey is shown to snatch a hearing aid from a nurse handing it to him; he then proceeds to swallow the hearing aid and comments that it needs more ketchup. This comic strip takes a current manifestation of the dominant pathologizing strategies and attacks it in a way that promotes self-worth. In doing so, it brings humor to a more general strategy to build self-worth by attacking the pathological dominance.

The hearing aid and, more recently, the cochlear implant symbolize age-old dominant practices to convert Deaf people into hearing people. While previously Deaf people sought to ward off pathological discourses by promoting the Deaf identity, current strategies essentially reverse the strategy: directly attacking symbols of pathology to promote identity. By celebrating the Deaf identity, the current strategies of confrontation blatantly denigrate the high value placed on the ability to hear.

Past internalization of such dominant discourses reinforced the status of Deaf people by stressing inabilities rather than abilities. Such reinforcement maligned their self-worth. The direct assault on these symbols of pathology, on the other hand, offers a rhetoric of self-worth within a culture of diversity. To embody this rhetoric of self-worth, practices such as the ceremonial destruction of hearing aids have been carried out by Deaf people at an international symposium in France ("The Future" 1990). Roslyn Rosen, vice-president for academic affairs at Gallaudet University and former president of the National Association of the Deaf, has also concluded that ears have usefulness as a resting place for her glasses (1991). Such declarations assert the wholeness of the Deaf being.

Consequently, the 1990 approval of the marketing of cochlear implants for children aged two to seventeen by the Food and Drug Administration has prompted a strong reaction in the post-Gallaudet Deaf social movement. Cochlear implants are a fairly recent development in the medical field in an attempt to restore or augment at least some residual hearing. The cochlear implant requires major surgery in which a hole is drilled into the skull to transplant the device. Children have been the primary focus for implantation, and this focus on children, who often are not in a position to make such critical decisions for themselves, is the reason for the reaction from Deaf adults. The value of cochlear implants for children is highly doubtful, because of its side effects, such as loss of balance, tinnitus, intense pain, and severe headaches (e.g., Roche 1991). Research has indicated very insignificant or no increases in the ability to understand words, particularly among "prelingually" Deaf children (Fryauf-Bertschy, Tyler, Kelsay and Gantz 1992; Osberger, Miyamoto, Zimmerman-Phillips, Kemink, Stroer, Firszt, and Novak 1991; Shea, Domico, and Lupfer 1994; Somers 1991; Waltzman, Cohen, Gomolin, Shapiro, Ozdamar, and Hoffman 1994).

The NAD has established a task force and developed a position paper condemning this "experimentation" on children as "ethically offensive" (Cochlear implants in children 1991, 1). Slogans have materialized to "stop the cochlear madness" or "if it's not broken, don't fix it" to denounce the spread of cochlear implants. So strong is the sentiment that cochlear implants are destructive to Deaf children, that parallels have been drawn to the Nazi regime. British scholar Paddy Ladd calls implants "the Final Solution" (Solomon 1994, 65). Deaf activist MJ Bienvenu explains, "Like the Nazis, they seem to enjoy experimenting on little children" (Solomon 1994, 65).

The symbolism of the cochlear implant has provoked such an intense reaction because it embodies the prevailing painful and torturous medicalizing strategies that many Deaf people have experienced, especially in childhood, to convert them into hearing, speaking people.[2] The cochlear implant is perceived as especially agonizing because unlike hearing aids that can be taken off on a whim, cochlear implants are surgically implanted. Deaf adults, after going through, in many cases, a difficult process to accept themselves as "Deaf," perceive the cochlear implant as an affront to their self-worth. Further, it is deemed offensive to their experiences, which suggest that the cochlear implant is simply an extension of the hearing aid and not likely to be of much help to most Deaf people. The central theme captured in the movement's response to the cochlear implant is that the hard-won battle for self-worth has become so precious that given a choice, many Deaf people would rather remain Deaf. As a Gallaudet student has avowed, "If there was a medication that could be given to deaf people to make them hear, I wouldn't take it. Never. Never til [sic] I die" (Karlen 1989, 134).

Not only has the Deaf social movement assaulted the rhetoric of pathology to reinforce the self-worth of the Deaf community, some discourse even turns the tables of pathology back to the dominant society. Deaf people label members of the dominant society much the same way that Deaf people have been labeled. Angela Stratiy, an ASL instructor, created a chart evaluating the skills of hearing people just learning to sign, assigning them such characteristics as "signing impaired," "hard-of-fingerspelling," "dexterity disabled," and other such labels (1989). These types of labels have often been applied to Deaf people by dominant discourses. This strategy by the Deaf movement is not limited to labels, however. Taking comments made by the dominant society and reversing the rhetoric to place Deaf people on the same level in the dominant hierarchy is a similar strategy. For instance, in response to a hearing mother who claimed the right to decide whether her Deaf child should be implanted on the basis that it "would make him more like [her], a hearing person," Gary Malkowski, a former Ontario legislator, replied: "Then presumably you have no objection to deaf parents requesting surgery to make their hearing child deaf" (cited in Lane 1992, 234). By creating a reversal in the rhetoric of pathology, such discourses by Deaf people illustrate a conscious refusal to be categorized according to dominant standards. By doing so, the sense of self-worth is validated.

The strategies to communicate a rhetoric of self-worth involve discourses of assertion, even confrontation, to attack prevailing discourses of pathology. Such a strategy, even though confrontational, validates the self-worth of the Deaf community. With this validation, the movement creates a discourse of difference, a rejection of the norm, and thus a celebration of diversity. Strategies of confrontation are more reminiscent of Black Power strategies than those of the diversity movements, however, in their rhetorical challenges to the dominant society. Even so, the rhetoric of self-worth serves a necessary function that enables the movement to work for the internal building of community and eventually toward a multicultural society.

Creating an Internal Foundation for Community Building

Within the family of cultural diversity strategies, the rhetoric of self-worth moves the social movement to a higher plane of challenging dominant discourses through themes that seek greater ownership of their community. African-centered curriculums and other multicultural practices illustrate this point. The Gallaudet movement embodied the ownership theme in the protesters' confrontation with patriarchal forces that had dominated the campus for years. The contemporary movement capitalizes on this theme by expanding it as a strategy to declare greater ownership within a multicultural framework.

One of the themes that characterized the rhetoric of Black Power was that the African American community was occupied— white people ran the community, administering it for those who lived there (Carmichael and Hamilton 1967). A central strategy in the post-Gallaudet movement has been the declaring of Deaf people's ownership of their community. The movement to place Deaf people in positions of authority in the community is illustrative of this strategy. The Gallaudet protest was a step in this direction. The theme of declaring ownership was exemplified at the Gallaudet protest in its demand for a Deaf president, as well as in its demand for a majority Deaf membership on the board of trustees. The successful launch of these demands at Gallaudet has paved the way for similar expectations elsewhere. This is illustrated in the number of Deaf superintendents of schools for the Deaf in the United States, which has grown to a total of twenty-two as of December 1995 (Deaf and hard of hearing superintendents of schools and programs for Deaf children 1995), compared with only four prior to the protest (Gannon, personal communication, December 5, 1991).

To ensure that the Gallaudet protest would not be a one-time thing, the Deaf social movement took advantage of the impetus to spread the discourses of Deaf ownership throughout the Deaf community. A particular focus for the strategy of Deaf ownership has been within the prevailing pathological practices of the educational establishment, where meager numbers of educators for the Deaf—approximately 10 to 20 percent—are themselves Deaf (e.g., Bahan 1989c; Coyne 1991).

The rhetoric of Deaf ownership is illustrated in Ben Bahan's proposal that the Deaf movement demand that for the next ten years, educational programs for the Deaf be restructured to accommodate a quota of at least 50 percent Deaf educators (1989c). The discourse of Deaf ownership has expanded from the call for increased Deaf people on the "outside" (e.g., the board) to that of the "inside" (e.g., a greater number of Deaf teachers).

The call for more Deaf teachers has been transformed into several rallies across the nation for increased Deaf ownership. The contemporary Deaf movement has also capitalized on the success of the Gallaudet protest by adopting rallies as occasions for communicating their demands. Additional examples of this practice include a protest held at the Wisconsin School for the Deaf in 1991 and at the Lexington Center, which includes the oldest school for the Deaf in New York, in 1994. The Wisconsin school protest bore resemblance to the Gallaudet protest in demands that the hearing dean of students be replaced with a Deaf person; that the then hearing superintendent be replaced with a Deaf person upon his anticipated retirement in 1993; a goal to hire enough Deaf people to compose a 51 percent Deaf staff at the school; and no reprisals against the students (Moering 1991b). The students' demands were met after two days of protests.

The Lexington protest also produced a "real sense of deja vu," according to Phil Bravin, who became the first Deaf chair of the Gallaudet University board of trustees as a result of the 1988 protest (Solomon 1994, 43). At Lexington, protesters objected to the process in which the new head, Max Gould, was selected, since the Deaf community had not been involved. The protesters demanded the ouster of Gould and involvement in the replacement process. The protest yielded successful results as well, with Gould's resignation, as well as receiving the same bonus that Gallaudet protesters received six years earlier—in the form of Phil Bravin as the new board chair (Solomon 1994).

These strategies explicitly convey the promotion of Deaf ownership. Less implicit is the relationship between Deaf ownership and access to the language of the Deaf community—ASL. John Shipman, then superintendent of the Wisconsin school, however, noted this connection: "In the deaf community in general, there's a movement toward bilingual and bicultural approach that also carries with it a belief that there should be a larger percentage of deaf employees. This thinking is developing, and our school is not the only place where that thinking is going on" (Deaf students push for change 1991, 1B). Similarly, Jackie Roth, one of the leaders of the Lexington protest, explains: "I didn't learn real A.S.L. until college and what a spreading of the wings it was when it happened! Lexington's tradition of arrogant oralism—they've got a lot to make up for" (Solomon 1994, 41). Indeed, the newer Deaf social movement has turned toward the strategy of other diversity movements to establish more control over their own community as a means to seek acceptance as a diverse culture with its own language.

The protesters at the Wisconsin school movement gained momentum during their protest by capturing the attention of the state department of education that has jurisdiction over the Wisconsin School for the Deaf. Assistant Superintendent of Schools Victor Contrucci, in representing the state department, legitimized the protesters' efforts to focus attention on their cultural and linguistic needs. Contrucci announced that his department was in contact with the state Department of Employment Relations to ask that civil service tests for candidates to the school incorporate consideration for users of ASL, as tests were typically given in standard English, presenting a potentially discriminatory situation against Deaf people (Moering 1991a). Further, affirmative action efforts would be examined to encourage the recruitment of more Deaf personnel to the school (Moering 1991a).

The protests at the Wisconsin and Lexington campuses are illustrative of the practice adopted by the Deaf social movement to target educational institutions as places to promote Deaf ownership. As places that foster the cultural community of Deaf people, educational institutions symbolize the home of Deaf people. And to ensure that these "homes" truly belong to Deaf people, it is necessary to establish ownership by placing them firmly under the control of Deaf people.

But administrative control is not the only aspect of ownership that has caught the current movement's attention. In addition, an old theme is back with increased intensity: the effort for full recognition of ASL as the language of the Deaf community. Where previously ASL was legitimized as a language outside the classroom, the newer movement brought it into the classroom in a fashion consistent with the multiculturalism cluster of rhetorical strategies. Consider, for example, the strategy to promote ASL through the rhetorical demand for a shift from "communication" to "language" policies in schools. Virtually every educational institution for Deaf students has communication policies that dominant discourses have long enforced, based on the premise that such policies serve as a guiding force for classroom communication. The movement's stress on "language policy" effectively shifts the focus of debate. No longer is the question: How will communication with the Deaf student in the classroom be best facilitated? Instead the question is posed: How will the language of the Deaf student best be facilitated?

The movement from communication to language policies has become a strategy to implement bilingual and multicultural approaches in the education of Deaf students. While the discourse of bilingualism promotes Deaf ownership, it also challenges the dominant society to take on a multicultural framework. In keeping with this strategy of the other diversity movements, Gallaudet students, two years after the Gallaudet protest, established an ASL Now campaign to rally for the recognition of ASL at Gallaudet. The students petitioned the Gallaudet faculty senate to "develop a language policy that officially recognizes American Sign Language and English as two official languages of Gallaudet University." Specifically, the students said, "We want Gallaudet to be a bilingual university" (Nye 1990, 5).

The push for language policies validates the bilingual and bicultural identity of Deaf people and condemns communication policies as a password or a "veiled term" (Valli 1990, 130) to legitimize the prevailing normalizing practices of Deaf people. This rhetorical move differs from the previous co-optive stance on total communication policies. The earlier struggle showed the acceptance of total communication as a way out from oralism even while it retained the theme of integration. The newer movement has brought the struggle into a different context. The shift to communication versus language policies creates a battle between integration and the preservation of cultural identity.

To support the argument that communication policies are normalizing practices, those making these arguments marshal evidence such as survey results showing that many teachers of Deaf students use sign and speech in the classroom, rather than adopting the tenets of the total communication philosophy (Woodward and Allen 1987). Others depict a "tower of Babel" scenario to portray total communication as a ridiculous practice. Bahan, for one, marshals support for a language policy with such a rhetorical strategy: "Imagine a teacher going over this sentence: George Washington never chopped down a cherry tree. Seven times for each child's need, using oral method, Rochester method (fingerspelling all the words in the sentence), SEE 2, writing, simultaneous method, drawing, and, if necessary for a child, Morse code. When the teacher finally finishes her sentence seven different times, it might be time for the child to go to another class" (Bahan 1989b, 119). Deaf people point to policies that enforce the use of speech as granting teachers permission to order signing Deaf students to "sit on your hands."

Even more "flexible" communication policies validate practices that require a conformity to the norm of speech. Simultaneous communication, for example, requires one to speak and sign at the same time. An editorial in the student newspaper at Gallaudet University illustrates how normalizing practices have been implicitly enforced by prevailing values placed on speech skills: "I find it strange that in the course of my school career, virtually all of the teachers and people that ask me to use my voice while signing are the ones who really suck dead dogs in sign language. These are the ones who ask me to speak for their —— ing benefit, while they don't make the slightest effort to improve THEIR signing" (Whetter 1989, 4).

Communication policies, however, not only promote normalizing practices of enforcing the standard modality and language on Deaf children, they have also become a strategy to legitimize discrimination against Deaf people. Deaf teachers who do not speak face employment discrimination, especially in the earlier grades where school policies stipulate the need for teachers to train Deaf children to speak. For instance, Beverly Hanyzewski, then a budding teacher, was denied an internship at a preschool program for the deaf because, according to the principal of the school: "[employees] must have good vocal skills, listening skills for evaluation of vocal skills" (Hanyzewski 1989, 3).

Many Deaf people have also related tales illustrating practices by educators to give lower grades to students who do not speak. Consequently, by ridiculing communication policies such as total communication, the movement targets language policies as a strategy to legitimize ASL in the classroom. Thus, language policies that recognize both ASL and English validate Deaf people's bilingual and multicultural status. Such policies encourage the acknowledgment of and respect for the cultural uniqueness of the Deaf community in keeping with the discourse of the diversity movements.

Further, this type of policy presents a rhetorical statement to the dominant society that Deaf people, as a distinct culture, should not be expected to function as the hearing people they are not. As a Deaf teenager aptly sums it up: "I'm deaf. Let me be deaf" (cited in Lane 1992, 238). A language policy, thus, creates the distinction between pathological and cultural practices. The Indiana School for the Deaf makes such a distinction: "The concept of bilingual/bicultural education for Deaf students is founded on a cultural perspective of Deaf life. This differs greatly from previous educational approaches that have been founded on a medical or pathological view of Deaf people, thus a bilingual/bicultural program represents a major shift in educational philosophy and attitude" (Bilingual/bicultural education 1990, 3).

The rhetoric of language policy, rather than communication policy, has begun its transformation into institutional practice at several programs. Bilingual programs have been established in various stages of advancement at the California School for the Deaf in Fremont, the Indiana School for the Deaf, the Learning Center for Deaf Children in Framingham, Massachusetts, the Maryland School for the Deaf, the Metro Deaf School in

Minneapolis, the Texas School for the Deaf, and the Wisconsin School for the Deaf. Other schools are currently exploring ways to facilitate this approach. Gallaudet has made a significant move toward this end with the establishment of a Deaf Studies department in 1994.

Strategies that promote Deaf ownership foster a strengthened internal foundation for community building. By this token, the Deaf movement adopts the strategy of "institutional" rather than "individualized" integration as presented by the diversity movements. Even though Deaf ownership is a form of separatist rhetoric, as the diversity proponents have argued, creating a discourse of self-worth and building a healthy foundation of ownership are actually necessary attributes for challenging dominant discourses of inequality. Declaring ownership is, thus, a strategy to invalidate discourses of inequality and consequently to promote a rhetoric of diversity in the dominant society.

Transforming the Internal Foundation to the External: Participation in Public Life

The Deaf-as-good phenomenon and the move toward greater control of the Deaf community serves the function of validating the self-defined perception of Deaf people as equal to their hearing peers. And by establishing a rhetoric of equality, Deaf people assert their right along with their hearing counterparts to participate in the public sphere. However, a rhetorical dilemma is faced by diversity movements, including the Deaf social movement, when dominant discourses posit the marginalized in a status of inequality.

For the Deaf community, a discourse of inequality has been created in the rhetoric of "It's a hearing world." Jane Bassett Spilman, former chair of the Gallaudet board of trustees, expressed it with the statement attributed to her that Deaf people are not ready to function in the "hearing world." Educators of the Deaf also prescribe the importance of speech skills and fluency in English because Deaf children live in a "hearing world." This rhetoric legitimizes a standard based on the norm of hearing people. Discrimination against Deaf people who do not speak, possess nativelike fluency in English, or subscribe to the cultural norms of the dominant society is validated based on the premise that they do not fit into a "hearing world." By accepting the ideological "It's a hearing world out there," Deaf people are placed in a subordinate position.

To counter this dominant practice, the Gallaudet protesters adopted a strategy of reversal: they responded with assertions that Zinser was not ready to function in the Deaf world. The post-Gallaudet movement has moved to a higher plane, however. Rhetoric such as "Hell, it's our world, too!" characterizes this newer strategy (Bahan 1989a, 47).

In line with multicultural rhetoric, the strategy of "It's our world, too" explicitly asserts the right of Deaf people to fully participate in public life. While the rhetoric of "It's a hearing world" compromises the self-worth of Deaf people and forces them to accommodate hearing standards, the newer strategy of assertion insists that society make accommodations for Deaf people. The integrationist position that adapting to societal norms is the only way for Deaf people to acquire full accommodation is challenged by Bahan, who stipulates that such an approach "will never work" (Bahan 1989a, 48). As some of the protesters of the Wisconsin protest point out, it "will never work," because "your [dominant society] world revolves around sound, ours revolves around sight—and that is why our language is so important to us. . . . You can learn our language, but we can never learn to hear" (Karlecke, Karlecke, Kelly, and Kelly 1991, 11). Alfred Sonnenstrahl, then executive director of Telecommunications for the Deaf, Inc., not only echoes similar rhetoric, but exhorts the Deaf community to adopt this strategy:

> Hearing people can learn to use their eyes and hands to communicate with deaf people through sign language. Deaf people cannot learn to use their ears to communicate with hearing people through hearing and speech. Deaf people should not be held responsible just because many hearing people choose not to exercise their option! Therefore, hearing people should assume the responsibility of bridging the communication gap. . . . Deaf people should use this and any other strategy to make sure that interpreters are provided, with no cost to them. Hearing

people have the option of learning sign language, but if they choose not to, it is their responsibility to find other alternatives that will facilitate communication. (Sonnenstrahl 1995, 4)

The strategy of "It's our world, too" thus insists that society accommodate the Deaf community in the move toward a multicultural society, because it will not work the other way around.

As a strategy to induce society to accommodate the Deaf community, the rhetoric of "communication abuse" (Mather and Mitchell 1994, 117) and "communication violence" (J. E. Tucker, personal communication, November 5, 1991)[3] has surfaced. Communication abuse is "abuse of a child through the refusal of a care-giver or teacher to provide a language, the provision of an inadequate language, or the failure to provide full access to communication" (Mather and Mitchell 1994, 120).

James Tucker, superintendent of the Maryland School for the Deaf, explains that the rhetoric of "communication violence" is a charge against dominant practices that do not fully accommodate the Deaf community. This covers a wide spectrum, ranging from the inability to communicate with nonsigning family members to the nonavailability of TTYs[4] at most telephone booths, to lack of access to intercoms and radios (J. E. Tucker, personal communication, November 5, 1991). The rhetoric of "communication abuse" and "communication violence" is thus a strategy to awaken the consciousness of both the Deaf community and the sensibilities of the dominant society. More significantly, however, strategies such as "It's our world, too," "communication abuse," and "communication violence" reject minimal accommodation and demand full participation in society. Bilingual proponents argue that it is language access that Deaf students need, not merely communication access. Accordingly, the rhetoric of "communication violence" is a demand for equal and total participation in the public sphere.

One recent strategy employs the rhetoric of "communication violence," evident in the transformation of a device that symbolized Deaf oppression into a symbol of diversity. Alexander

Graham Bell left behind a legacy that would present an insur-
mountable barrier toward participation in public life for Deaf
people—the telephone. The telephone has for years legitimized
discriminatory practices against Deaf people, especially in employment. Even in Deaf establishments, virtually every institution
has made it a practice to hire at least one hearing employee to
answer voice calls. Such a policy focuses on what Deaf people
cannot do, rather than what they can do.

Consequently, some Deaf people have chosen to target the
telephone as the symbol that obstructs full public participation.
The choice of the telephone as a symbol is a bold strategic move.
With the Gallaudet movement, the rhetoric of Deaf ownership
was played out through the strategy of claiming turf that should
officially have belonged to the Deaf community. The newer
strategy of the telephone, on the other hand, is a brazen move to
turn an object held dear by the dominant society into an object
that legitimizes discriminatory practices against Deaf people. The
telephone is pointed to as a symbolic obstruction to full public
participation, since the practice of hiring hearing people to
answer voice calls sends the message that there are indeed some
things Deaf people are not able to do, even within their own
establishments. And if they cannot perform these functions in
their own community, then employers outside Deaf establishments are justified in not hiring Deaf people, because they cannot
fulfill these crucial roles.

As such, declaring the telephone to be a symbol of discrimination has prompted Deaf people such as Jack Levesque to propose
that programs and services providing services to Deaf people enact
policies to accept only TTY calls (1991). At least one agency, the
Abused Deaf Women's Advocacy Services (ADWAS) in Seattle,
Washington, has put this strategy into practice ("We are not"
1996, 13). This strategy requires voice callers to access establishments with such a policy via a telephone relay system,[5] and thus
places the telephone, which has long legitimized employment
discrimination against Deaf people, in a subordinate position.

The proposal to ban voice calls would also alter the technology of communication, opening up very different rhetorical possibilities. By reversing the roles, with non-TTY callers at the receiving end having to adopt technologies, this strategy serves to place these callers in a subordinate role. Most of these callers, presumably hearing people, will then experience what Deaf people go through every day of their lives in placing calls to people who do not have TTYs. In this vein, the condemnation of the telephone promotes self-worth by validating the Deaf-as-good motif and establishes the right to full involvement in public life, thus creating an environment for greater tolerance of cultural diversity.

This strategy of the newer Deaf movement appears to create a paradox—seeking greater public participation by refusing to communicate using the dominant technology of the very society the community is trying to participate in. However, this strategy shows the power of cultural diversity strategies—marginalized groups rejecting access on terms that deny their identity. This is shown in the practice of the transformation of self-worth and a strong sense of community into public participation built with bridges to diversity rather than with access as inferior members—marginal members of the broader public community. Rather than seeking integration, as exemplified by the practice of accommodating on society's terms, this strategy demands full and equal participation on their own terms. Such a strategy also mocks an old nemesis—Alexander Graham Bell—recaptured in a different mode.

For the Deaf social movement, demands that society adapt to Deaf people are also tempered by an invitation to work together to achieve that goal. The movement to officially recognize ASL as a language across the nation is such a strategy. As Bahan contends, since Deaf people cannot conform to society, the dominant society can and should accommodate the Deaf community (1989a). One way to make this possible is to teach them ASL.[6] Today, many states have legislation recognizing ASL as an official language, and a growing number of high schools and universities offer classes for credit.

The Deaf movement has also recognized the importance of raising the consciousness of the dominant society. Examples, to name a few, include calls for libraries to expand their offerings of materials illustrating cultural views of the Deaf community (Hagemayer 1993; Mather 1992); the increasing entry of Deaf cultural experiences into the dominant society, for example, in literature with books such as *Deaf in America: Voices from a Culture* by noted researchers Carol Padden and Tom Humphries; in videotapes such as the *ASL Literature Series: Bird of a Different Feather & For a Decent Living* by storytellers Ben Bahan and Sam Supalla; in the media, as in *Sesame Street;* and in art that integrates signs into the scenery, as seen in artist Chuck Baird's work (Baird 1993). Publishers who specialize in ASL and Deaf culture literature, such as Joe Dannis of DawnSignPress, recognize the importance of reaching out to the dominant society: "With the increased interest in American Sign Language (ASL), curiosity about Deaf culture has grown, and so has Deaf people's pride in it. As a Deaf publisher, I have a mission to preserve our Deaf heritage for this generation and the next" (Baird 1993, preface).

One especially important new strategy for educating the dominant society is the growth of Deaf Studies programs. Boston University, California State University at Northridge, the University of Arizona, and most recently, Gallaudet University have Deaf Studies departments. Many schools across the country have implemented Deaf Studies courses or materials into their programs. A curriculum guide, *The KDES Deaf Studies Curriculum Guide,* has been developed for elementary-age students. While the Deaf movement has primarily hailed Deaf Studies as a way to validate their language and culture, to strengthen their identity, and to foster self-worth and pride in their heritage (Kannapell 1992), Deaf Studies is also a strategy to educate the dominant society. Harvey Corson, former Gallaudet University provost and current superintendent of the Kentucky School for the Deaf, explains that "new knowledge . . . must have an outlet, a means by which the information can be transmitted to the world," and therefore, "all of us, deaf and hearing, will ultimately benefit from this work, and by collaboratively discovering and sharing knowledge, we will more fully recognize the richness of our diversity as well as our similarities as human beings" (Corson 1992, 11).

Another outgrowth of Deaf Studies programs is the strategy of empowerment. Deaf Studies programs can pave the way for an increased number of Deaf scholars. Deaf scholars will contribute significantly to an enhanced understanding of the Deaf community by bringing to studies a "unique insight, intuition and creative imagination to the process of discovery, theorizing, and dissemination" (Lane, Hoffmeister, and Bahan 1996, 442), thus creating a cycle of empowerment. The more Deaf scholars participate in their own research, the more they learn, and the more society learns. Because Deaf people best know their own needs and, therefore, are the best spokespersons for their own causes, the strategy of empowerment has the potential to create greater awareness and understanding of Deaf causes in the dominant society.

In keeping with the strategy of empowerment, the establishment of a "barrier-free environment" is argued to have far-reaching implications in that it can empower Deaf students who "would learn the full meaning of access and apply that awareness to their future lives in the wider society" (Jankowski 1995, 1). Indeed, the Deaf movement is increasingly adopting the strategy of empowerment to ensure fuller participation of present and future generations of Deaf people in the world that belongs to both Deaf and hearing people.

Diversity movements share the belief that offering a multicultural education will enable the dominant society to better understand and thus respect various cultures. Accordingly, the movement to teach ASL as a recognized language—analogous to "foreign" languages common in our society, such as Spanish—in addition to broadening the consciousness of the dominant society and empowering future generations of Deaf people, is a strategy toward creation of a pluralistic society. For the Deaf social movement, the official recognition of ASL throughout the country would validate its bilingual and multicultural status. Acknowledging ASL as a language and educating the dominant society about Deaf culture would promote a humanistic image of the Deaf community as a cultural and linguistic entity and put to rest the predominately pathological view of Deaf people. The movement to officialize ASL and promote Deaf culture fosters an environment that is willing to accommodate diversity and is, then, a strategy to create a pluralistic America.

Conclusion

Traditionally, rhetorical studies become interested in describing the full diffusion and effects of rhetorical strategy. The strategies described in this chapter are contemporary strategies. They have not reached their full potential, nor have the effects of their power been witnessed. Nevertheless, the rhetorical scholar can see their use and application to the Deaf movement and community.

For instance, a dilemma that has just begun to be addressed by the Deaf social movement involves the balance between separatism and assimilation. Is there even a need for such a balance? As separatist rhetoric argues, total assimilation will not work because it deprives the cultural individual of his or her cultural identity. For Deaf people, full assimilation is not possible since society does not accommodate the basic communication needs of Deaf people. On the other hand, integrationists contend that total separatism is not possible for economic survival. As the three proposed attributes for community building indicate, a solution would appear to be a fusion of the best elements of each faction.

This theory is substantiated by Killian and Grigg, who discuss a similar dilemma in regard to the assimilation of African Americans into society (1964). They argue that for assimilation to work, African Americans need to have a psychologically and mentally healthy regard for themselves so that white people will be dealing with people who have a positive sense of their history and of themselves as whole beings. This evaluation need not be restricted to African Americans. Such a diagnosis can extend to other cultural groups, including Deaf Americans. In societies that deem certain groups of people, such as Deaf people, as not normal, strategies are needed to modify dominant perceptions. A positive sense of self-worth, internal community building, and full participation in public life have become strategies for maintaining a distinctive cultural identity.

Like other diversity movements, in recent years the Deaf movement has created new strategies to address prevailing themes. The newer strategies exemplify a strengthened rhetoric of self-assertion as evidenced by the transformations of jokes, the condemnation of the fixation on the ear, and mockery of the pathological labeling of Deaf people. These strategies pose a stark contrast to earlier co-optive practices. The increased rhetoric of self-assertion lends credence to arguments that social movements pave the way toward empowerment among the membership as they break from traditional patterns and move to create further changes (e.g., A. King 1987).

This study of the rhetorical shaping of empowerment for the cultural identity of the Deaf movement resembles the position taken by Black Power advocates. Creating a sense of self-worth gives the marginalized group a sense of self-pride and thus generates a new cycle of assertive rhetoric among the membership. With this healthy regard for themselves as a cultural identity, members become empowered to establish a greater stake in their territory, which in turn increases their self-worth and pride. Staking out a larger territory emboldens and empowers the members to approach the dominant society from an equal, rather than a marginal, position. Since the dominant society has created the rhetoric of pathology, demeaning marginalized groups, empowerment must come from within. Black Power takes this position, as do the contemporary diversity movements, and in turn, as this book illustrates, the Deaf movement has begun to move in this direction as well.

The earlier practices of the Deaf social movement, enhanced by the successful Gallaudet protest, thus validated and strengthened the power of self-worth and presented new opportunities to create collective ownership and demands for full involvement in public life. A break in the vicious cycle of pathologic rhetoric has occurred, but is not yet complete. Consequently, the Deaf social movement is continuing the work begun by chipping further away at that break. This practice is demonstrated in the promotion of bilingual and multicultural approaches, for instance, to reinforce self-worth and to establish opportunities for greater control over their own establishments.

The strategy of retaining a separate cultural identity not only creates the basis for a healthy foundation, it also presents a means by which the cultural group can participate in the public sphere as an equal, rather than a subordinate. That is the strategy of diversity—to promote a strong foundation by which cultural groups retain their identity and are respected for their identity, while being extended the invitation to become equal partners in society.

Notes

1. Hearing aids are "assistive devices" that help people use their residual hearing to pick up environmental sounds and to improve their word discrimination so they can better understand speech. However, for a great number of Deaf people, hearing aids serve little or no use.

2. Medicalizing strategies include hearing aids, listening devices worn by Deaf students with gigantic earphones while the teacher wears a microphone, and other similar devices to thrust the burden of developing speech and listening faculties on all Deaf children.

3. James Tucker coined the term after an inspiration from the Reverend Jesse Jackson, who frequently speaks a rhetoric of "diversity." Jackson had employed the term *economic violence* to refer to the failure of the government to distribute equally to its constituents. He argued that all Americans should have basic health care at a very minimum, as the present system offers the best health care to those who can afford it. As a result, innocent children suffer from this practice, thus, the institution of "economic violence."

4. *TTY* is the original abbreviation for teletypewriter, a device used by Deaf people to communicate via the telephone. Both parties must possess a TTY for this communication to be possible. The TTY has a keyboard and a small screen. The two parties type messages back and forth.

5. Telephone relay systems refer to the process in which Deaf people communicate with people who do not have access to a TTY, and vice versa. The

consumer of this service can call it using either a TTY or telephone, and "opera-tors" are the third party who translate calls between the caller and the person called.

6. A poll in *Deaf Life* magazine suggests overwhelming support for hearing people to learn ASL (96 percent). Among some of the comments: "More barri-ers between the hearing and non-hearing communities will fall." "Hearing people [would gain] . . . a better understanding of the Deaf, [besides] . . . they see the Deaf more often than foreigners." And, "DEFINITELY! Then more hearing people will feel comfortable talking to & [*sic*] meeting Deaf people" ("Readers' Viewpoint" 1989, 31).

7

Conclusion

This book began as an examination of the Deaf social movement's rhetorical strategies to shape empowerment of its cultural identity. Such a study brings a new understanding of the role social movements play in the empowerment of not only the Deaf community, but of other marginalized groups as well. The uniqueness of the communication modality used by Deaf people also brought on a status that distinguished it from other marginalized groups. As a result, in the case of the Deaf social movement, communication is not merely the means, but is the issue itself. This phenomenon presents a vision of a different world for communication. The first section of this conclusion will focus on what has been learned about social movements and their treatment by rhetorical scholars. The second will address what has been learned about the Deaf social movement.

Toward a Theory of Empowerment in Social Movements

The study of social movements by rhetorical scholars is still a relatively new area of research, affording rich opportunities to contribute to the field. The dominant theory of social movements has tended to treat these movements as marginalized groups trying to establish access to the dominant society. Such an approach is basically an integrationist theory of appeal. Social movements are, thus, studied from the perspective of the marginal trying to access the dominant society by persuading the dominant to allow them to do so, rather than from the perspective of encouraging society to accept diversity.

As this study of the Deaf social movement has illustrated, studying social movements within a framework of empowerment and Foucault's characterization of the normalizing process brings out a new dimension of social movements. Such a treatment places social movements as a powerful force challenging the dominant society to create change by accommodating marginalized peoples. This approach to studying movements brings on an understanding of how the process of empowerment not only creates the impetus for a social movement, but sustains and expands a cycle of empowerment that reaches out to marginalized members and increases from one generation to the next. This understanding of the role of empowerment explains how each generation of marginalized groups becomes emboldened and, thus, more willing to challenge the dominant society.

In the application of a theory of empowerment to the Deaf social movement, we were able to see how the conflicting pressures of dominance and resistance played out through the historical struggle of the Deaf community and the dominant society. Even as dominant themes of normalization repeatedly prevailed throughout the years, the Deaf movement was able to resist by creating counterstrategies. These counterstrategies increased in strength and assertiveness as more Deaf people adopted strategies to create pride in themselves. The struggles between the dominant and dominated were illustrated as they played themselves out from one generation to the next, increasing in intensity, and as themes repeated themselves in new contexts, as, for example, in pathologic discourses that first forced oralism on the Deaf community, then later returned in stronger force, as surgical implants.

By studying these stages in the Deaf movement through a theory of empowerment, we were able to appreciate the efforts of the movement to build an internal community. In this vein, the integrationist approach to the study of movements restricts, in that a narrow frame of access to the dominant society overshadows the research, and significant strategies for empowerment may be overlooked. This suggests that studies of social movements would benefit from a theory of empowerment to escape from integrationist inclinations.

Using Foucault's depiction of the normalizing process to study movements fits in well with a theory of empowerment. For one thing, a Foucaultian approach helps us understand the position of social movements as they challenge the normalizing pattern so ingrained in the dominant society. Beyond that, the rhetorical construct of normality helps us understand how movements become marginalized by rhetorical studies based on the assumption that movements seek access to society. The perception of the dominant society as "normal" has inadvertently created a parallel expectation that movements, in representing the "deviant," seek access to the "normal." So implicit is this practice that rhetorical scholars have accepted this integrationist approach as the norm. By using a Foucaultian approach, this tendency becomes clear and thus becomes a useful guide in preventing such tendencies.

In addition to the empowerment and Foucaultian frame of study, the treatment of the Deaf social movement in this book is a departure from previous studies in one other way. Traditionally, movements have been studied synchronically—by isolating them in their particular point in time. The treatment of the Deaf movement has, on the other hand, spanned a time period of over a hundred years. Making this study diachronic has proved illuminating for a number of reasons. An examination of the historical events of the movement provides a means for comparison of strategies and has allowed us to learn how these strategies adapted over time. In this study, for instance, we were able to see the emergence of empowerment as the cycle shifted over the years from strategies of co-optation to strategies of confrontation. Addressing the various stages as the movement evolved has also brought us a better understanding of how current strategies are adopted and how they compare to strategies of other movements over time. We were thus able to discern how the other liberating movements and societal trends influenced the strategies of the Deaf movement. Further, this approach allows us to look at the whole picture and at the common links among the phenomena. Without addressing the historical context of the movement, for example, the emergence of a Deaf identity, the demand for a Deaf president at Gallaudet University, and current diversity strategies might be misunderstood.

The Deaf Movement

The previous chapter showed that the necessary attributes for community building include creating a sense of self-worth, building an internal foundation for community building, and seeking full participation in the public sphere. This theory of community building presents a vision of multiculturalism as a strategy for a different world of communication. The question then arises: Can the rhetorical world envisioned by multiculturalism succeed?

The Multicultural Community

Roslyn Rosen describes what a "Utopia" for Deaf people would be like:

> There would be no difference in education, employment, communications and community life. . . . There would be total access, around the clock, on television, in movie theatres, over the phone, and in any human interactions. . . . There would be captions and signers everywhere. . . . Programs serving deaf people would be managed by deaf people. In the absence of attitudinal barriers, paternalism would fly out the window. There would be total acceptance of a multicultural society and valuing of natural differences in people. There would be true partnerships between deaf and non-deaf people in all walks of life. (Rosen 1990, 3)

Is such a society possible? Documented evidence of societies in which Deaf people are perceived as normal suggest that it is. Studies of these societies indicate that "normality" is a culturally constructed practice that results in an environment that fosters a more successful assimilation for Deaf people than has been evident in

America and elsewhere. Indeed, there have been reports and studies of assimilation that have occurred or are thriving in the following communities: Little Cayman Island (Doran 1952); Ayent, a Swiss commune (Secretan 1954; Hanhart 1962); Katwijk, a Dutch village (Aulbers 1959); the Lancaster County, Pennsylvania Amish and Mennonites (Mengel, Konigsmark, Berlin, and McKusick 1967; McKusick 1978); a clan of Jicaque Indians in the Honduras (Chapman and Jacquard 1971); Adamarobe, a village in Ghana (David, Edoo, Mustaffah, and Hinchcliff 1971); the Guntar area of Andhra Pradesh in India (Majumdar 1972); Urubu, Brazil; a Scottish clan, Jewish communities in Britain (Fraser 1976); cultural units in Israel (Costeff and Dar 1980); a Mayan Indian village of Nohya (Shuman 1980); villages of Providence Island in the Caribbean (Washabaugh 1979; Woodward 1982); Martha's Vineyard in Massachusetts (Groce 1985); and the Yucatec Mayan village in Mexico (Frishberg 1987).

The significance of these communities is that the society accommodated Deaf people, rather than the other way around. On Martha's Vineyard, for instance, beginning in the 1700s and continuing for over two hundred years, many hearing people used sign language in their daily interactions because of the high number of Deaf inhabitants. The residents were so accustomed to using sign language that it was treated as a way of life for the inhabitants—hearing and Deaf (Groce 1985). This ability to interact without hindrance carried over to the perception of Deaf people by the hearing residents. When one informant was asked how the Deaf residents were perceived, the response was: "Oh, they [hearing residents] didn't think anything about them, they were just like everybody else" (Groce 1985, 2). Even though Martha's Vineyard and most of these communities were small, making it easier to accommodate diversity, the fact that the phenomenon of assimilation occurred at all is evidence that Deaf people (or other diverse groups) can be accommodated by a dominant society.

Further, these studies suggest that a willingness to accommodate a cultural group corresponds to its perception of the group as "normal." This thesis is substantiated by a study of Providence Island, where the number of Deaf residents is two to three times higher than average. Sociolinguist James Woodward concluded in his survey of hearing informants on the island that more positive attitudes were generally held about their Deaf residents than were held by hearing people of Deaf people in the United States (1982). For instance, in the United States, dominant discourses have assumed that Deaf people are pathologically deficient.[1] In contrast, Woodward found that 77 percent of the hearing informants on the island determined that Deaf people are equally as intelligent as, or more intelligent than, their hearing peers, and equally mature (81 percent) (1982). In regard to employment, Deaf people in the United States are victimized by pervasive discrimination practices.[2] Hearing Providence Islanders were more receptive, however, to hiring Deaf people, although the motivation to do so was diminished at the time of the survey because of economic problems on the island. Nevertheless, pay scales were equal between Deaf and hearing people, unlike the situation in the United States.

Another difference in the perception of sign language was also apparent.[3] Of the hearing islanders, only one person believed that Providence Island Sign Language was brought to Deaf residents from outsiders; 11 percent gave credit to hearing people for developing the sign language of Deaf islanders, and only 14 percent believed sign language was universal. Additionally, 77 percent of the hearing islanders believed Providence Island Sign Language was grammatical, and 63 percent of them regarded sign language as a different language from their spoken language. Most significantly, a strong majority (79 percent) maintained that hearing people should learn sign language to communicate with Deaf people, rather than Deaf people learning to speak in order to communicate with the dominant society.

Much can be gleaned from these studies. Certainly there is a relationship between how a society defines people who differ from the norm and their reaction toward such people. These studies suggest a positive relationship between a dominant society that adapts to its diverse populations and their perceptions of equality. In view of these results, the proposed theory of community building appears warranted. Since the perception of "normality" is culturally constructed by dominant societies, the theory of community building presents a strategy to modify these firmly held dominant constructs.

The Status of the Deaf Movement

This brings us to the question of how the Deaf social movement has fared thus far in the move toward a multicultural society. As compared with other marginalized groups, one may be forced to concede that Deaf people have not come as far as other movements in making dents in the prevailing pathological perceptions held by the dominant society. Although the Deaf social movement has made inroads in making Deaf people more visible and in generating a greater sense of awareness about their community in the dominant society, much ignorance remains.

Other movements for the most part are represented by spokespersons who are members of their cultural community. European Americans are rarely featured as mouthpieces for African Americans, nor for that matter do men speak for the women's movement. Most African American and women's groups, as well as other cultural groups, predominate within their own establishments and hold decision-making power. Dominant discourses, while still a discourse of inequality in regard to the structural hierarchy, have undergone a transformation that for the most part restricts such discourse to a subtle level.

Deaf people, on the other hand, are more often than not represented in the media by hearing people who present themselves as experts on the Deaf community. While making strides, especially since the successful Gallaudet protest, in placing Deaf people in authoritative positions, the progress toward that end remains a gradually emerging process, and has yet to reach the levels of representation evident in other nondominant controlled establishments. Dominant discourses, while seeking to be helpful, continue to unconsciously adopt blatantly paternalistic tones in addressing the issues of the Deaf community.

This slow progress of the Deaf social movement in comparison to other marginalized movements does not indicate the ineffectiveness of the strategies used by Deaf people, however. When evaluating the strategies used by the Deaf community thus far, it is necessary to note that the Deaf movement is restricted by barriers that may prove far more pervasive than is apparent in other movements. For one thing, most Deaf people are not born into their community. This creates an automatic gap not problematic in most movements, with the possible exception of the lesbian and gay movement. Accordingly, Deaf people take longer to create coalition. Further, additional barriers, such as mainstreaming or inclusion, prevent most Deaf people from readily entering the Deaf community. Adapting to the Deaf community requires a period of adjustment, and this process must be completed before a Deaf person can begin to warm up to the Deaf social movement.

For another thing, the paradox that Deaf people face of being classified into one category with all disabled people can place the Deaf movement at a disadvantage. To align with the disability movement is to ensure the provision of access and the protection of human rights for Deaf people. These are rights that the Deaf movement reveres. On the other hand, the primary goal of the disability movement—full integration—seeks to destroy the homes of Deaf people, the "segregated" residential schools for the Deaf. This creates a serious rhetorical challenge for the Deaf movement, in that they will not only be challenging dominant discourses, but the disability community that they are perceived to be a part of, as well. If the Deaf movement disassociates itself from the disability movement, their numbers are smaller, and thus, their political force diminished.

Additionally, the number of people actively participating in the

Deaf social movement may be much smaller than in other move-ments. This is compounded by the pervasive divisions within the Deaf community.[4] Further, the modality of speech holds reigning power almost universally. This modality so pervasively separates Deaf people from society that it creates a situation in which soci-ety resorts to gleaning information about the Deaf community through people who share their modality. Thus, the modality difference makes it easy for hearing people to maintain symbolic and literal control over Deaf people.

In view of these barriers unique to the Deaf social movement, the Deaf community has indeed come a long way in asserting its rights and empowering its community. To further advance their cause, the Deaf social movement should take into account the added rhetorical barriers they face and strategize to resolve these dilemmas. For instance, they should acknowledge that the rhetor-ical barriers Deaf people face in American society are so pervasive that the dominant culture perceives the Deaf cultural community as deviant and therefore, the movement toward Deaf ownership as especially threatening. The Deaf social movement might, as a case in point, consider these factors in its struggle to enact bilin-gual and multicultural programs in schools. This move may be perceived as intimidating, especially to people not fluent in the language or culture of Deaf people. It need not be. Granted, the increasing prominence of ASL in educational institutions and other establishments may impose greater demands on employees who do not possess fluency in ASL and legitimize a hiring system that favors Deaf people.

However, bilingualism and multiculturalism can actually em-power both Deaf and hearing people. Since ASL symbolizes the status of Deaf people as equal to, yet distinct from, hearing people, the dominant society will be forced to reexamine its per-ception of the Deaf community. Further, the increased visibility of Deaf people as coworkers will improve the fluency of their hearing peers' ASL skills, which usually correlates with the amount of interaction made with the cultural group. By being in close proximity with Deaf adults, hearing people would be given greater opportunity to interact with Deaf people. Frequent association with Deaf people is also likely to reduce the "mystery" of Deaf culture and to create a perception of Deaf people as their equals.

Along with this view of Deaf people as "peers" is the potential for greater respect for them. Respecting Deaf people also means valuing their views and their experiences, and consequently trusting them in leading their own community. And if Deaf people are trusted to create environments where other Deaf people are allowed to maximize their abilities and to accept their Deaf identity, the self-image that develops is far more healthy. People with healthier self-images are more likely to relate well to other people. Thus, Deaf people who are brought up in positive environments where their Deaf identity is valued, are likelier candidates for full and equal participation in the public sphere. As Killian and Grigg argue, a lasting solution for assimilation is not for African Americans to pass as white, but to explore the meaning of being "American" (1964). As long as being American implicitly denotes being white, it will remain difficult for African Americans to have equal standing as Americans. By the same token, for assimilation to become effective for Deaf people and other marginalized groups, society needs to examine its ideology of "normality."

To address these rhetorical dilemmas, the proposed theory of community building may prove inadequate. There is a need also to allay the fears of members of the dominant society. This may well be the fourth attribute for the vision of a multicultural society. Even if the three attributes were fully accomplished, inequalities could still prevail. If care is not taken, previous oppressors may simply be placed in the role of the oppressed. The fourth element, thus, needs to be the discourse of "humanitarianism." This may be the most difficult criterion, yet a necessary one, in order to achieve a more egalitarian society. The struggle to break free from the constraints of oppression may place the oppressed in a position to penalize the former oppressors for their long-term suffering. This process serves only to continue the vicious cycle. Such a cycle can only be broken by establishing new prece-dents. Coalition building may be such a precedent. The discourse of humanitarianism embraces the oppressors and strives for a more equal society—but only after the oppressed have built up the foundation that enables them to reach this stage.

The diversity movements in the United States appear to be a step in the right direction. Consider, for instance, a report submit-ted by a government task force on Native American education to the U.S. Department of Education promoting the provision of a "multi-cultural environment" (Cooper 1991, A19). In response to the high dropout rate of Native American students from public schools (only 10 percent attend tribal schools on Native reserva-tions), the following are among the recommendations made. Schools should "offer Native students the opportunity to main-tain and develop their tribal languages and [schools] will [then be able to] create a multicultural environment that enhances the many cultures represented in the school" (A19). The number of Native American educators should be doubled. Existing Native preschool programs and tribal colleges should be strengthened to improve education for Native students.

Similarly, the Deaf social movement has come a long way in empowering its people and in striving for a more equal partner-ship with their hearing counterparts. The rhetorical strategies of the Deaf social movement are empowering in the implications for a more pluralistic society. After all, these strategies draw society away from the "melting pot" ideology, which restricts in that it encourages conformity to the norm, in favor of pluralism, which respects and celebrates diversity. The practice of pluralism em-powers because it accommodates American democratic ideals and enables everyone equal respect regardless of differences.

Notes

1. Woodward (1982) cites a review of thirty-eight major studies over a thirty-seven-year span, demonstrating that it was a common occurrence to find hearing people in the United States equating a Deaf person's intelligence with

his or her speech ability, regardless of the person's actual level of intelligence (Mindel and Vernon 1971). Even hearing educators of Deaf students have shown a tendency to pathologize the behaviors of Deaf people.

2. Rickard, Triandis, and Patterson found that personnel directors were more willing to hire people with tuberculosis or in wheelchairs than Deaf people (1963). These directors were only more receptive to hiring Deaf people than people with epilepsy, ex-convicts, or former mental patients. However, when it came to the hiring of third-grade teachers, Deaf people were placed last, next to people with epilepsy (cited in Woodward 1982).

3. Dominant discourses in the United States often posit that sign language was brought to Deaf people, rather than its being a natural phenomenon (Woodward 1982). Woodward also indicates the mistaken belief of many Americans that ASL is an universal sign language, not realizing that each country possesses its own sign language (Battison and Jordan 1976). Further, many Americans (both hearing and Deaf) have constituted ASL as a broken or ungrammatical language (see Woodward 1982, for sources). This study has also illustrated the overall preference as constructed in dominant discourses for oral skills over sign language.

4. The Deaf community, as delineated in Chapter 5, has traditionally faced internal divisions, including Deaf oralists, ASL users, those from mainstreamed schools, those from residential schools, African Americans, and so on.

References

Adam, B. D. 1987. *The rise of a gay and lesbian movement*. Boston: Twayne.

Amman, J. C. 1873. *A dissertation on speech*. Translated by J. Baker. London: Sampson Low, Marston, Low, and Searle.

Arensberg C., and A. Niehoff. 1964. *Introducing social change: A manual for Americans overseas*. Chicago: Aldine.

Aristotle. 1910. *History of animals*. Edited and translated by J. A. Smith and W. D. Ross. Oxford: Clarendon Press.

Arnez, N. L., and C. B. Anthony. 1968. Contemporary negro humor as social satire. *Phylon* 22:339–46.

Aulbers, B. J. M. 1959. *Erfelijke aangeboren doofheid in Zuid-Holland* [Inherited deafness from birth in South Holland]. Delft, Holland: Waltman.

Bahan, B. 1989a. It's our world too! In *American deaf culture*, edited by S. Wilcox. Silver Spring, Md.: Linstok Press.

———. 1989b. Total communication: A total farce. In *American deaf culture*, edited by S. Wilcox. Silver Spring, Md.: Linstok Press.

———. 1989c. The war is not over. In *American deaf culture*, edited by S. Wilcox. Silver Spring, Md.: Linstok Press.

Baird, C. 1993. *Chuck Baird: 35 plates*. San Diego, Calif.: DawnSignPress.

Baker, C. 1978. How does "sim-com" fit into a bilingual approach to education? In *Proceedings of the Second National Symposium on Sign Language Research and Teaching*, edited by F. Caccamise and D. Hicks. Silver Spring, Md.: National Association of the Deaf.

———. 1983. A microanalysis of the non-manual components of questions in ASL. Ph.D. diss., University of California, Berkeley.

Baker, C., and C. Padden. 1978. *American Sign Language: A look at its history, structure, and community*. Silver Spring, Md.: T. J. Publishers.

Baker-Shenk, C. 1986. Characteristics of oppressed and oppressor peoples: Their effect on the interpreting context. In *Interpreting: The art of cross-cultural mediation,* edited by M. McIntire. Silver Spring, Md.: RID Publications.

Ballin, A. 1930. *The deaf mute howls.* Los Angeles: Grafton.

Banner, L. W. 1980. *Elizabeth Cady Stanton: A radical for women's rights.* Boston: Little, Brown.

Barnhart, J. S. 1991. The transition process of hearing-impaired new sign language freshmen: An interview study of first semester experiences at Gallaudet University. Ph.D. diss., Gallaudet University, Washington, D.C.

Battison, R., and I. K. Jordan. 1976. Cross cultural communication with foreign signers: Fact and fancy. *Sign Language Studies* 10:53–68.

Beckwith, C. 1988. Expression of Deaf pride. *Buff and Blue,* March 4, p. 7.

Bell, A. G. 1883. *Memoirs upon the formation of a deaf variety of the human race.* New Haven: National Academy of Sciences.

Bender, R. 1970. *The conquest of deafness.* Cleveland: Press of Case Western Reserve University.

Berger, P. L., and T. Luckmann. 1966. *The social construction of reality.* New York: Doubleday.

Best, H. 1943. *Deafness and the deaf in the United States.* New York: Macmillan.

Bilingual/bicultural education: Philosophy statement. 1990. *Bi-Cultural News,* April–May, pp. 1–3.

Bittner, E. 1963. Radicalism and the organization of radical movements. *American Sociological Review* 28:928–40.

Blumer, H. 1969. Social movements. In *Studies in social movements: A social psychological perspective,* edited by B. McLaughlin. New York: Free Press.

Bookman, A., and S. Morgen, eds. 1988. *Women and the politics of empowerment.* Philadelphia: Temple University Press.

Booth, E. 1858. Letter to J. J. Flournoy in "Mr. Flournoy's Plan for a Deaf-Mute commonwealth." *American Annals of the Deaf and Dumb* 10:40–42.

Bosmajian, H. 1983. *The language of oppression.* Lanham, Md.: University Press of America.

———. 1992. Defining the "American Indian": A case study in the language of suppression. In *Exploring language,* edited by G. Goshgarian. 6th ed. New York: HarperCollins Publishers.

Bourdieu, P. 1990. *Outline of a theory of practice.* Translated by R. Nice. Cambridge: Cambridge University Press.

Brasel, K., and S. P. Quigley. 1977. The influence of certain language and communication environments in early childhood on the development of language in deaf individuals. *Journal of Speech and Hearing Research* 20:95–107.

Brockriede, W. E., and R. L. Scott. 1968. Stokely Carmichael: Two speeches on black power. *Central States Speech Journal* 19:3–13.

Bruske, E. 1988. Protest gained empathy nationwide. *Washington Post*, March 11, p. A16.

Burke, K. [1945] 1969. *A grammar of motives*. 2d ed. Berkeley: University of California Press.

———. [1941] 1973. *The philosophy of literary form: Studies in symbolic action.* 3d ed. Berkeley: University of California Press.

Campbell, K. K. 1971. The rhetoric of radical black nationalism: A case study in self-conscious criticism. *Central States Speech Journal* 22:151–60.

———. 1983. Femininity and feminism: To be or not to be a woman. *Communication Quarterly* 31(2): 101–8.

———. 1986. Style and content in the rhetoric of early Afro-American feminists. *Quarterly Journal of Speech* 72: 434–45.

———. 1989. *Man cannot speak for her: A critical study of early feminist rhetoric* (Vol. 1). New York: Praeger.

Carlson, A. C. 1992. Creative casuistry and feminist consciousness: The rhetoric of moral reform. *Quarterly Journal of Speech* 78: 16–32.

Carmichael, S. 1966. Toward black liberation. *Massachusetts Review* 7:639–51.

Carmichael, S., and C. V. Hamilton. 1967. *Black power: The politics of liberation in America*. New York: Vintage Books.

Castle, D. L. 1990. Employment bridges cultures. In *Eyes, hands, voices: Communication issues among Deaf people: A Deaf American monograph*, edited by M. Garretson, pp. 19–21. Silver Spring, Md.: National Association of the Deaf.

Cathcart, R. S. 1978. Movements: Confrontation as rhetorical form. *Southern Speech Communication Journal* 43:233–47.

Chamberlain, W. M. 1857. Proceedings of the second convention of the New England Gallaudet association of deaf-mutes. *American Annals of the Deaf and Dumb* 9:65–87.

———. 1858. Proceedings of the third convention of the New England Gallaudet association of deaf-mutes. *American Annals of the Deaf and Dumb* 10:205–19.

Chapman, A. C., and A. M. Jacquard. 1971. Un isolate d'Amerique Centrale: les Indiens Jicques de Honduras en *Genetique et population: Hommage a Jean Sulter* [A focus on Central America: The Jicques Indians of Honduras. In *Genetics and population: In honor of Jean Sulter*, pp. 163–85]. Paris: I.N.E.D.

Chesebro, J. W., J. F. Cragan, and P. McCullough. 1973. The small group technique of the radical revolutionary: A synthetic study of consciousness-raising. *Speech Monographs* 40:136–46.

———. 1981. Consciousness-raising among gay males. In *Gay speak: Gay male and lesbian communication*, edited by J. W. Chesbro. New York: Pilgrim Press.

Christiansen, J. B., and S. N. Barnartt. 1995. *Deaf president now! The 1988 Revolution at Gallaudet University*. Washington, D.C.: Gallaudet University Press.

Cochlear implants in children: A position paper of the National Association of the Deaf. 1991. *NAD Broadcaster,* March, p. 3.

Cometor, J. 1988. Reverse discrimination? [Letter to the editor]. *Buff and Blue,* March 4, p. 5.

Conrad, C. 1981. The transformation of the "old feminist" movement. *Quarterly Journal of Speech* 67:284–97.

Coogan, M. 1996. Revised curriculum proposal passes. *On the Green,* November 21, pp. 1, 4.

Cooper, K. J. 1991. Multicultural focus recommended for education of native Americans. *Washington Post,* December 27, p. A19.

Corson, H. 1973. Comparing deaf children of oral deaf parents and deaf children using manual communication with deaf children of hearing parents on academic, social, and communicative functioning. Ph.D. diss., University of Cincinnati.

———. 1992. Deaf studies: A framework for learning and teaching. In *Deaf Studies for Educators*. Washington, D.C.: Gallaudet University.

Corson denies statement. 1988. *Buff and Blue,* March 11, p. 3.

Costeff, H., and H. Dar. 1980. Consanguinity analysis of congenital deafness in northern Israel. *American Journal of Human Genetics* 32:64–68.

Covington, V. C. 1980. Problems of acculturation into the deaf community. *Sign Language Studies* 28:267–85.

Coyne, J. 1991. No more voice calls? [Letter to the editor]. *DCARA News,* March–April, p. 13.

Crandall, K. 1974. A study of the production of chers and related language aspects by deaf children between the ages of three and seven years. Ph.D. diss., Northwestern University, Evanston, Ill.

Crittendon, J. 1986. Attitudes toward sign communication mode: A survey of hearing and hearing-impaired educators of the deaf. *American Annals of the Deaf* 131:275–80.

Daly, M. 1978. *Gyn/ecology: The metaethics of radical feminism.* Boston: Beacon Press.

David, J. B., B. B. Edoo, F. O. Mustaffah, and R. Hinchcliff. 1971. Adamarobe—a "deaf" village. *Sound* 5:70.

Deaf and hard of hearing superintendents of schools and programs for Deaf children. 1995. Washington, D.C.: Gallaudet University, National Information Center on Deafness.

Deaf protesters heard; new president named. 1988. *Bay City Times,* March 14, p. A1.

Deaf students push for change. 1991. *Janesville Gazette,* November 18, p. 1B.

DeLoach, M. B. 1990. Identity and social movements: The student protests at Gallaudet University. Ph.D. diss., University of Southern California, Los Angeles.

DeLorenzo, K. 1988. Students: Deaf president now! *Buff and Blue,* March 4, pp. 1, 3.

Denton, D. M. 1972. A rationale for total communication. In *Psycholinguistics and total communication: The state of the art,* edited by T. J. O'Rourke. Washington, D.C.: American Annals of the Deaf.

Derrida, J. 1976. *Of grammatology.* Translated by G. Spivak. Baltimore: Johns Hopkins University Press.

Doctor, P., ed. 1962. Directory of services for the deaf [Special issue]. *American Annals of the Deaf,* p. 107.

Dodd, C. H. 1987. *Dynamics of intercultural communication.* 2d ed. Dubuque, Iowa: W. C. Brown.

Donovan, J. 1985. *Feminist theory: The intellectual traditions of American feminism.* New York: Frederick Ungar.

Doran, E., Jr. 1952. Inbreeding in an isolated island community. *Journal of Heredity* 43:263–66.

Douglas, M. 1968. The social control of cognition: Some factors in joke perception. *Man* 3:361–76.

Dozier, J. 1988. Hear no evil. *AGB Reports,* July/August: pp. 6–18.

Duncan, H. D. 1962. *Communication and social order.* New York: Bedminster Press.

Ebonics plan altered. 1997. *Washington Post,* 17 January, p. A6.

Edwards, A. D. 1976. *Language in culture and class: The sociology of language and education.* London: Heineman Educational Books.

Elsasser, N., and V. P. John-Steiner. 1977. An interactionist approach to advancing literacy. *Harvard Educational Review* 47:355–69.

Elshtain, J. B. 1979. *Public man, private woman.* Princeton: Princeton University Press.

Erting, C. 1982. Deafness, communication, and social identity: Analysis of interactions among parents, teachers, and deaf children in a preschool. Ph.D. diss., American University, Washington, D.C.

Faculty minutes. 1988. Special meeting, March 9 [Minutes of the University Faculty]. Gallaudet University, Washington, D.C.

Farb, P. 1974. *Word play: What happens when people talk?* New York: Alfred Knopf.

Fay, E. A. 1882. Tabular statement of the institutions of the deaf and dumb of the world. *American Annals of the Deaf and Dumb* 27:32–53.

———. 1896. An inquiry concerning the results of marriages of the deaf in America. *American Annals of the Deaf* 41:79–88.

———. 1900. The Paris Congress of 1900. *American Annals of the Deaf* 45: 404–16.

Fine, G. A. 1983. Sociological approaches to the study of humor. In *Handbook of humor research,* edited by P. E. McGhee and J. H. Goldstein. New York: Springer-Verlag.

Fiske, J. 1987. British cultural studies and television. In *Channels of discourse,* edited by R. Allen. Chapel Hill: University of North Carolina Press.

Flournoy, J. J. 1856. Scheme for a commonwealth of the deaf and dumb. *American Annals of the Deaf and Dumb* 8:118–25.

———. 1858. Reply to objections. *American Annals of the Deaf and Dumb* 10:140–51.

Foss, S. K. 1989. *Rhetorical criticism: Exploration and practice.* Prospect Heights, Ill.: Waveland Press.

Foucault, M. 1970. *The order of things: An archaeology of the human sciences.* Translated by A. Sheridan. New York: Pantheon Books.

———. 1977. *Discipline and punish: The birth of the prison.* Translated by A. Sheridan. New York: Pantheon Books.

———. 1978. *The history of sexuality: An introduction.* Vol. 1. Translated by R. Hurley. New York: Pantheon Books.

———. 1980. *Power/knowledge: Selected interviews and other writings, 1972–1977.* Edited by C. Gordon. Translated by C. Gordon, L. Marshall, J. Mepham, and K. Soper. New York: Pantheon Books.

Fraser, G. R. 1976. *The causes of profound deafness in childhood.* Baltimore: Johns Hopkins University Press.

Freire, P. 1970. *Pedagogy of the oppressed.* Translated by M. B. Ramos. New York: Seabury Press.

Frishberg, N. 1987. Sign languages: Ghanaian. In *Gallaudet encyclopedia of deaf people and deafness,* edited by J. V. Van Cleve. New York: McGraw-Hill.

Fryauf-Bertschy, H., R. S. Tyler, D. Kelsay, and B. J. Gantz. 1992. Performance over time of congenitally and postlingually deafened children using a multi-channel cochlear implant. *Journal of Speech and Hearing Research* 35:913–20.

The future society of the deaf. 1990. *TBC News,* September, p. 1.

Gallaudet, E. M. 1881. The Milan convention. *American Annals of the Deaf* 26:1–16.

Gallaudet, E. M., and P. Hall. 1909. The normal department of Gallaudet College [and sign in instruction]. In *Proceedings of the Convention of American Instructors of the Deaf,* pp. 38–56.

Gannon, J. R. 1981. *Deaf heritage: A narrative history of deaf America.* Silver Spring, Md.: National Association of the Deaf.

——. 1989. *The week the world heard Gallaudet.* Washington, D.C.: Gallaudet University Press.

Garretson, M. 1980. Foreword. In *Sign Language and the deaf community: Essays in honor of William C. Stokoe,* edited by C. Baker and R. Battison. Silver Spring, Md.: National Association of the Deaf.

Geer, S. 1986. Public law 94-142: A summary of decisions affecting hearing impaired children. *Gallaudet Today* [Special issue], pp. 31–35.

Genovese, E. 1972. *Roll, Jordan, roll: The world the slaves made.* New York: Vintage.

Giroux, H. 1983. *Theory and resistance in education: A pedagogy for the opposition.* South Hadley, Mass.: Bergin and Garvey.

Goffman, E. 1963. *Stigma: Notes on the management of spoiled identity.* New York: Simon and Schuster.

Gregg, R. 1971. The ego-function of the rhetoric of protest. *Philosophy and Rhetoric* 4:71–91.

Griffin, L. M. 1952. The rhetoric of historical movements. *Quarterly Journal of Speech* 38:184–88.

——. 1966. A dramatistic theory of the rhetoric of movements. In *Critical responses to Kenneth Burke: 1924–1966,* edited by W. H. Rueckert. Minneapolis: University of Minnesota Press.

Groce, N. E. 1985. *Everyone here spoke sign language: Hereditary deafness on Martha's Vineyard.* Cambridge: Harvard University Press.

Gurko, M. 1976. *The ladies of Seneca Falls: The birth of the woman's rights movement.* New York: Schocken Books.

Hagemayer, A. L. 1993. Looking to the future: A librarian's perspective. *Deaf American* 43:33–38.

Halliday, M. A. K. 1978. *Language as a social semiotic.* Baltimore: University Park Press.

Hamilton, C. V. 1968. An advocate of black power defines it. *New York Times Magazine,* April 14, pp. 22–23, 79–83.

Handler, M. S. 1966. Wilkins says Black Power leads only to Black death. *New York Times,* July 6, pp. 1, 14.

Hanhart, E. 1962. *Die genealogische und otologische Erforschung des grossen Walliseer Herdes von rezessiver Taubheit und Schwehorigkeit im Laufe der letzten 30 Jahre (1933–1962)* [The genealogical and orthogenetic investigation of whale pods for recessive deafness and hearing impairment over the last 30 years (1933–1962)]. Arch. Klaus-Stift Vereb-Forsh.

Hanyzewski, B. 1989. Too bad to be true: Deaf teacher unqualified to teach deaf pre-schoolers. *TBC News,* June, pp. 3–4.

Harrington, W. 1991. Black & white & Spike all over. *Washington Post Magazine,* June 2, pp. 11–27.

Harris, T. L. 1982. Desegregation vs. mainstreaming: Commendable goals, questionable processes. In *Deaf people and social change,* edited by A. Boros and R. Stuckless (Working Papers No. 6, pp. 151–75). Washington, D.C.: Gallaudet College Research Institute.

Hartman, A. 1881. *Deaf mutism and the education of deaf-mutes by lip-reading and articulation.* Translated by J. P. Cassells. London: Bailliere, Tindall and Cox.

Hawkesworth, M. E. 1990. *Beyond oppression: Feminist theory and political strategy.* New York: Continuum.

Higgins, P. C. 1988. *Outsiders in a hearing world: A sociology of deafness.* Beverly Hills, Calif.: Sage.

Hodgson, K. W. 1954. *The deaf and their problems.* New York: Philosophical Library.

Houston, P. 1988. Students' victory is symbol for deaf. *Los Angeles Times,* March 12, p. 1–2.

Humphries, T. 1975. *The making of a word: Audism.* Unpublished manuscript.

Hymes, D. 1962. The ethnography of speaking. In *Anthropology and human behavior,* edited by T. Gladwin and W. C. Sturtevant. Washington, D.C.: Anthropological Society of Washington.

Hymowitz, C., and M. Weissman. 1978. *A history of women in America.* New York: Bantam.

Jacobs, L. M. 1974. *A deaf adult speaks out.* Washington, D.C.: Gallaudet College Press.

Jaggar, A., and P. Rothenberg. 1978. *Feminist frameworks: Alternative theoretical accounts of the relations between men and women.* New York: McGraw-Hill.

Jankowski, K. 1991. On communicating with deaf people. In *Intercultural communication: A reader,* edited by L. A. Samovar and R. E. Porter, 6th ed. Belmont, Calif.: Wadsworth.

———. 1995. Quality education for deaf and hard of hearing students: What it takes. *DSD/HH Insider,* March, pp. 1–2.

Japp, P. M. 1985. Esther or Isaiah?: The abolitionist-feminist rhetoric of Angelina Grimke. *Quarterly Journal of Speech* 71:335–48.

Johnson, R. E., S. K. Liddell, and C. J. Erting. 1989. Unlocking the curriculum: Principles for achieving access in deaf education (Working Paper 89-3). Washington, D.C.: Gallaudet University Research Institute.

Johnstone, M. 1988. In my opinion: Views about the Gallaudet revolution. *Gallaudet Today,* Summer, pp. 26–29.

Jones, J. 1918. One hundred years of history in the education of the deaf in America and its present status. *American Annals of the Deaf* 63:1–47.

Jones, R. L. 1989. What's wrong with black English. In *Exploring language,* edited by G. Goshgarian. 5th ed. Glenview, Ill.: Scott, Foresman.

Jordan, I. K. 1988. Statement by I. King Jordan [press release], March 10. Gallaudet University, Washington, D.C.

Jordan, I. K., G. Gustason, and R. Rosen. 1979. An update on communication trends at programs for the deaf. *American Annals of the Deaf* 124:350–57.

Jordan, I. K., and M. A. Karchmer. 1986. Patterns of sign use among hearing impaired students. In *Deaf children in America,* edited by A. N. Schildroth and M. A. Karchmer. San Diego: College-Hill Press.

Jordan, J. 1981. *Civil wars.* Boston: Beacon Press.

Kannapell, B. 1974. Bilingual education: A new direction in the education of the deaf. *Deaf American* 26:10, pp. 9–15.

———. 1992. The role of deaf identity in deaf studies. In *Deaf Studies for Educators,* edited by J. Cebel. Washington, D.C.: Gallaudet University College of Continuing Education.

———. 1993. *Language choice—Identity choice.* Burtonsville, Md.: Linstok Press.

Karlecke, J., R. Karlecke, S. Kelly, and D. Kelly. 1991. In support of WSD superintendent responds to protest [Letter to the editor]. *Delavan Enterprise and Delavan Republican,* November 28, pp. 10, 11.

Karlen, N. 1989. Louder than words. *Rolling Stone,* March 23, pp. 134–40.

Killian, L. M., and C. Grigg. 1964. *Racial crisis in America.* Englewood Cliffs, N.J.: Prentice-Hall.

King, A. 1987. *Power and communication.* Prospect Heights, Ill.: Waveland Press.

King, M. L. 1967. *Where do we go from here: Chaos or community?* New York: Harper and Row.

Klima, E., and U. Bellugi. 1979. *The signs of language.* Cambridge: Harvard University Press.

Kluwin, T. 1981. A preliminary description of the control of interaction in classrooms using manual communication. *American Annals of the Deaf* 126:510–14.

Koppel, T., host. 1988. *Nightline.* Deaf students protest (Transcript Show No. 1773). New York: ABC News.

Kramarae, C. 1981. *Women and men speaking: Frameworks for analysis.* Rowley, Mass.: Newbury House.

Kriesberg, L. 1973. *The sociology of social conflicts.* Englewood Cliffs, N.J.: Prentice-Hall.

Lakoff, R. T. 1990. *Talking power: The politics of language in our lives.* New York: Basic Books.

Lane, H. 1980. A chronology of the oppression of sign language in France and the United States. In *Recent perspectives on American Sign Language,* edited by H. Lane and F. Grosjean. Hillsdale, N.J.: Lawrence Erlbaum.

———. 1984. *When the mind hears.* New York: Random House.

———. 1985. On language, power, and the deaf. In *Proceedings of the 1985 Interpreters for the Deaf Convention,* edited by M. L. McIntire. Silver Spring, Md.: RID Publications.

———. 1992. *The mask of benevolence: Disabling the deaf community.* New York: Alfred A. Knopf.

Lane, H., R. Hoffmeister, and B. Bahan. 1996. *A journey into the deaf-world.* San Diego: DawnSignPress.

Lee, R. 1992. Pride and confidence. In *Deaf liberation,* edited by R. Lee. England: National Union of the Deaf.

Leibowitz, A. 1976. Language and the law: The exercise of political power through official designation of language. In *Language and politics,* edited by W. O'Barr and J. O'Barr. Paris: Mouton.

Lentz, E. 1995. The door. In *The Treasure: Poems by Ella Mae Lentz.* Berkeley: InMotion Press.

Levesque, J. 1991. No more voice calls at DCARA? *DCARA News,* February, p. 2.

Littlejohn, S. 1989. *Theories of human communication.* 3d ed. Belmont, Calif.: Wadsworth.

Long, J. S. 1918. *The sign language: A manual of sign.* Omaha, Nebr.: Dorothy Long Thompson.

Lou, M. W. 1988. The history of language use in the education of the deaf in the United States. In *Language learning and deafness,* edited by M. Strong. Cambridge: Cambridge University Press.

Lowy, J. L. 1988. In support of "Gallaudet's presidential selection travesty" [Letter to the editor]. *Washington Post,* March 12, p. A24.

McCrone, W. P. 1991. Equality under the law. *Gallaudet Today,* Spring, pp. 14–18.

McGee, M. C. 1980. "The ideograph": A link between rhetoric and ideology. *Quarterly Journal of Speech* 66:1–16.

McGuire, M. 1977. Mythic rhetoric in Mein Kampf: A structuralist critique. *Quarterly Journal of Speech,* 63:1–13.

McKusick, V. A. 1978. *Medical genetic studies of the Amish: Selected papers.* Baltimore: Johns Hopkins University Press.

Majumdar, M. K. 1972. Preliminary study on consanguinity and deaf mutes. *Journal of the Indian Medical Association* 58:78.

Making employment accessible to deaf persons: Section 504, A law to stop discrimination against disabled persons. 2d ed. 1981. Washington, D.C.: Gallaudet University, National Center for Law and the Deaf.

Marmor, G., and L. Petitto. 1979. Simultaneous communication in the classroom: How well is English grammar represented? *Sign Language Studies* 23:99–136.

Martineau, W. H. 1972. A model of the social functions of humor. In *The psychology of humor,* edited by J. H. Goldstein and P. E. McGhee. New York: Academic Press.

Marx, K., and F. Engels. 1972. *The German ideology,* edited by C. J. Arthur. New York: International Publishers.

Mather, S. 1990. Is America really a free country for us all? In *Eyes, hands, voices: Communication issues among Deaf people: A Deaf American monograph,* edited by M. Garretson, pp. 87–89. Silver Spring, Md.: National Association of the Deaf.

———. 1992. How pathological and cultural views of deafness affect service-delivery programs. In *Deaf Studies: What's Up?.* Washington, D.C.: Gallaudet University.

Mather, S., and R. Mitchell. 1994. Communication abuse: A sociolinguistic perspective. In *Post Milan ASL and English Literacy: Issues, Trends and Research,* edited by B. Snider. Washington, D.C.: Gallaudet University Continuing Education and Outreach.

Meadow, K. P. 1967. The effect of early manual communication and family climate on the deaf child's development. Ph.D. diss., University of California, Berkeley.

———. 1968. Early manual communication in relation to the deaf child's intellectual, social, and communicative functioning. *American Annals of the Deaf* 113:29–41.

Mengel, M. C., B. W. Konigsmark, C. I. Berlin, and V. A. McKusick. 1967. Recessive early-onset neural deafness. *Acta Oto-laryngologica* 64:313–26.

Mentkowski, S. C. 1985. Trends in 1984–85 state legislation. *Gallaudet Today,* Spring, p. 28.

Merrill, E. C. 1988. Letter to Jane Bassett Spilman, February 26.

Mindel, E. D., and M. Vernon. *They grow in silence: the deaf child and his family.* 1971. Silver Spring, Md.: National Association of the Deaf.

Moering, H. 1991a. WSD students protest lack of deaf on staff. *Delavan Enterprise and Delavan Republican,* November 19, pp. 1, 7.

——. 1991b. Dean reassigned, WSD protest ends. *Delavan Enterprise and Delavan Republican*, November 21, pp. 1, 16.

Moores, D. F. 1978. *Educating the deaf: Psychology, principles, and practices.* Boston: Houghton Mifflin.

Multra, C. 1988a. DPN bull session in cafe: Students plan for 2nd rally. *Buff and Blue,* March 4, p. 6.

——. 1988b. The beginning: Sunday. *Buff and Blue,* March 9, pp. 2, 5.

Munoz, L. 1991. Maryland deaf residents protest 911 delay. *Washington Post,* July 10, p. B7.

National Education Association. 1885. Proceedings of meeting held in the Senate Chamber, Madison, Wisconsin, July 16, 1884, to Consider the Subject of Deaf-Mute Instruction in Relation to the Work of Public Schools. Washington, D.C.: Gibson.

Nover, S. 1995. Politics and language: American Sign Language and English in deaf education. In *Sociolinguistics in deaf communities,* edited by C. Lucas. Washington, D.C.: Gallaudet University Press.

Nye, E. 1990. Student's signature . . . *ASL Now Newsletter,* April 23, p. 5.

Oates, S. B. 1982. *Let the trumpet sound: The life of Martin Luther King, Jr.* New York: Harper and Row.

O'Neill, W. 1971. *Everyone was brave: A history of feminism in America.* Chicago: Quadrangle Books.

Osberger, M. J., R. T. Miyamoto, S. Zimmerman-Phillips, J. L. Kemink, B. Stroer, J. B. Firszt, and M. A. Novak. 1991. Independent evaluations of the speech perception abilities of children with the Nucleus-22 channel cochlear implant system. *Ear and Hearing Supplement* 12(4):66S–80S.

Padden, C., and T. Humphries. 1988. *Deaf in America: Voices from a culture.* Cambridge: Harvard University Press.

Padden, C., and H. Markowicz. 1976. Cultural conflicts between hearing and deaf communities. In *Proceedings of the Seventh World Congress of the World Federation of the Deaf,* edited by F. B. Crammatte and A. B. Crammette. Silver Spring, Md.: National Association of the Deaf.

Pearse, C. G. 1912. The oral teaching of the deaf. *Nebraska Journal* 40:2–3.

Pfeiffer, J. 1989. Girl talk–boy talk. In *Exploring language,* edited by G. Goshgarian. 5th ed. Glenview, Ill.: Scott, Foresman.

Philp, M. 1985. Michel Foucault. In *The return of grand theory in the human sciences,* edited by Q. Skinner. Cambridge: Cambridge University Press.

Pianin, E., and M. Sinclair. 1988. Congressman urges Zinser to resign. *Washington Post,* March 10, pp. A1, A20–21.

Piccolli, S. 1988. Gallaudet rally calls for deaf president. *Washington Times,* March 2, pp. B1, B3.

Pooley, R. C. 1989. The definition and determination of "correct" English.

In *Exploring language,* edited by G. Goshgarian. 5th ed. Glenview, Ill.: Scott, Foresman.

Position statement on full inclusion. 1994. Silver Spring, Md.: National Association of the Deaf.

Pre-college teachers urged to sign without voice, use ASL in class. 1991. *On the Green,* September 9, p. 1.

Quigley, S. P., and P. V. Paul. 1984. ASL and ESL? *Topics in Early Childhood Special Education* 3:17–26.

Rainer, J. D., and W. E. Deming. 1963. Demographic aspects: Number, distribution, marriage, and fertility statistics. In *Family and mental health problems in a deaf population,* edited by J. D. Rainer, K. Z. Altshuler, and F. J. Kallman. New York: New York State Psychiatric Institute.

Readers' Responses: Have you personally experienced discrimination because you're deaf? 1994. *Deaf Life,* September, p. 28.

Readers' Viewpoint: Do you think that Deaf people have equal rights in the United States? 1988. *Deaf Life,* September, p. 31.

Readers' Viewpoint: Should ASL be offered in high school and college for foreign-language credit? 1989. *Deaf Life,* April, p. 31.

Reich C., D. Hambleton, and B. K. Houldin. 1977. The integration of hearing impaired children in regular classrooms. *American Annals of the Deaf* 122:534–43.

Rickard, T. E., E. C. Triandis, and C. H. Patterson. 1963. Indices of employer prejudice toward disabled applicants. *Journal of Applied Psychology* 47:52–55.

Rider, H. C. 1877. Elmira convention of deaf mutes. *American Annals of the Deaf and Dumb* 22:251–52.

Rimlinger, G. V. 1970. The legitimation of protest: A comparative study in labor history. In *Protest, reform, and revolt: A reader in social movements,* edited by J. R. Gusfield. New York: John Wiley and Sons.

Rittenhouse, R. K., C. Johnson, B. Overton, S. Freeman, and K. Jaussi. 1991. The black and deaf movements in America since 1960. *American Annals of the Deaf* 136:392–400.

Roche, K. 1991. Little more than noise. *TBC News,* October, p. 5.

Rodda, M. 1982. An analysis of the myth that mainstreaming and integration are synonymous. In *Deaf people and social change,* edited by A. Boros and R. Stuckless (Working Papers No. 6, pp. 121–49). Washington, D.C.: Gallaudet College Research Institute.

Rodriguez, R. 1989. Aria: A memoir of a bilingual childhood. In *Exploring language,* edited by G. Goshgarian. 5th ed. Glenview, Ill.: Scott, Foresman.

Rosen, R. 1990. The president signs on. *NAD Broadcaster,* December, p. 3.

———. 1991. The president signs on. *NAD Broadcaster,* February, p. 3.

Ross, M. 1978. Mainstreaming: Some social considerations. *Volta Review* 80:21–30.

———. 1990. Definitions and descriptions. In *Our forgotten children: Hard of hearing pupils in the schools,* edited by J. Davis. 2d ed. Bethesda, Md.: Self Help for Hard of Hearing People.

Rutherford, S. D. 1989. Funny in deaf—not in hearing. In *American deaf culture,* edited by S. Wilcox. Silver Spring, Md.: Linstok Press.

Sacks, O. 1989. *Seeing voices: A journey into the world of the deaf.* Berkeley: University of California Press.

Samovar, L. A., and R. E. Porter. 1991. *Communication between cultures.* Belmont, Calif.: Wadsworth.

Sanchez, C. 1988. Gallaudet students: "We want ours!" *Washington Post,* March 8, p. A12.

Sanchez, R. 1996. Oakland school system recognizes "Black English" as a second language. *Washington Post,* December 20, p. A8.

———. 1997. Ebonics: A way to close the learning gap? *Washington Post,* January 6, p. A1.

Sarachild, K. 1970. A program for feminist "consciousness raising." *Notes from the second year: Women's liberation, major writings of the radical feminists,* pp. 76–84. New York: Radical Feminism.

Saville-Troike, M. 1989. *The ethnography of communication: An introduction.* 2d ed. New York: Basil Blackwell.

Schein, J. D. 1989. *At home among strangers.* Washington, D.C.: Gallaudet University Press.

Schein, J. D., and M. T. Delk. 1974. *The deaf population of the United States.* Silver Spring, Md.: National Association of the Deaf.

Schuchman, J. S. 1988. *Hollywood speaks: Deafness and the film entertainment industry.* Urbana: University of Illinois Press.

Schulz, M. 1984. Minority writers: The struggle for authenticity and authority. In *Language and power,* edited by C. Kramarae, M. Schulz, and W. M. O'Barr. Beverly Hills, Calif.: Sage.

Scott, R. L. 1968. Justifying violence—the rhetoric of militant black power. *Central States Speech Journal* 19:96–104.

Scott, R. L., and W. Brockriede. 1969. *The rhetoric of black power.* New York: Harper and Row.

Scott, R. L., and D. K. Smith. 1969. The rhetoric of confrontation. *Quarterly Journal of Speech* 55:1–8.

Secretan, J. P. 1954. *De la surdi-mutité recessive et de ses rapports avec les autres formes de surdi-mutité* [On recessive deaf-muteness and its relation to other forms of deaf-muteness]. Arch. Klaus-Stift VererbForsch.

Shapiro, J. 1991. In search of a word for (shhh!) disabled. *Washington Post,* August 25, p. C4.

———. 1994. *No pity: People with disabilities forging a new civil rights movement.* New York: Times Books, Random House.

Shea, J. J., E. H. Domico, and M. Lupfer. 1994. Speech perception after multichannel cochlear implantation in the pediatric patient. *American Journal of Otology* 15:66–70.

Shuman, M. K. 1980. Culture and deafness in a Maya Indian village. *Psychiatry* 43:359–70.

Simons, H. W. 1972. Persuasion in social conflicts: A critique of prevailing conceptions and a framework for future research. *Speech Monographs* 32:227–47.

Sinclair, M. 1988a. 1,500 at Gallaudet urge "Deaf President Now." *Washington Post,* March 2, pp. B1, B7.

———. 1988b. Students close Gallaudet U. *Washington Post,* March 8, pp. A1, A12.

Sinclair, M., and E. Pianin. 1988. Protest may imperil Gallaudet funding. *Washington Post,* March 9, pp. A1, A11.

Smith, P. 1970. *Daughters of the promised land: Women in American history.* Boston: Little, Brown.

Smitherman, G. 1977. *Talkin and testifyin: The language of black America.* Boston: Houghton Mifflin.

———. 1989. White English in blackface, or who do I be? In *Exploring language,* edited by G. Goshgarian. 5th ed. Glenview, Ill.: Scott, Foresman.

Smith-Rosenberg, C. 1975. The female world of love and ritual: Relations between women in nineteenth-century America. *Signs* 1:1–30.

Snyder, B. 1988. *Language, communication and English—Defining one's terms.* Washington, D.C.: Gallaudet University, Department of Linguistics and Interpreting. Unpublished manuscript.

Solomon, A. 1994. Deaf is beautiful. *New York Times Magazine,* August 28, pp. 40–45, 62, 65–68.

Solomon, B. B. 1976. *Black empowerment: Social work in oppressed communities.* New York: Columbia University Press.

Solomon, M. 1988. Ideology as rhetorical constraint: The anarchist agitation of "Red Emma" Goldman. *Quarterly Journal of Speech* 74:184–200.

Somers, M. N. 1991. Speech perception abilities in children with cochlear implants or hearing aids. *American Journal of Otology* 12:174–78.

Sonnenstrahl, A. 1995. It is up to the hearing to ensure full communication. *Silent News,* February, p. 4.

Spradley, J. P. 1979. *The ethnographic interview.* New York: Holt, Rinehart and Winston.

——. 1980. *Participant observation*. New York: Holt, Rinehart and Winston.

Stein-Schneider, H. 1988. In support of Gallaudet's presidential selection travesty [Letter to the editor]. *Washington Post,* March 12, p. A24.

Stewart, C. J., C. A. Smith, and R. E. Denton, Jr. 1989. *Persuasion and social movements.* 2d ed. Prospect Heights, Ill.: Waveland Press.

Stokoe, W. C., Jr. 1960. Sign language structure: An outline of the visual communication system of the American deaf. *Studies in Linguistics* (Occasional Papers No. 8). State University of New York at Buffalo, Department of Anthropology and Linguistics.

Stratiy, A. 1989. The real meaning of "hearing impaired." *TBC News,* November, p. 1.

Stuckless, E., and J. Birch. 1966. The influence of early manual communication on the linguistic development of deaf children. *American Annals of the Deaf* 111:425–60, 499–504.

Tannen, D. 1990. *You just don't understand: Women and men in conversation.* New York: William Morrow.

Toch, H. 1965. *The social psychology of social movements.* New York: Bobbs-Merrill.

Trenholm, S. 1991. *Human communication theory.* 2d ed. Englewood Cliffs, N.J.: Prentice-Hall.

Valli, C. 1990. A taboo exposed: Using ASL in the classroom. In *Eyes, hands, voices: Communication Issues Among Deaf People: Deaf American Monograph,* edited by M. Garretson, pp. 129–31. Silver Spring, Md.: National Association of the Deaf.

Van Cleve, J. V., and B. A. Crouch. 1989. *A place of their own: Creating the deaf community in America.* Washington, D.C.: Gallaudet University Press.

Veditz, G. 1913. *Preservation of the sign language* [film]. Silver Spring, Md.: National Association of the Deaf.

Vernon, M., and S. Koh. 1970. Effects of manual communication on deaf children's educational achievement, linguistic competence, oral skills, and psychological development. *American Annals of the Deaf* 115:527–36.

Waltzman, S. B., N. L. Cohen, R. H. Gomolin, W. H. Shapiro, S. R. Ozdamar, and R. A. Hoffman. 1994. Long-term results of early cochlear implantation in congenitally and prelingually deafened children. *American Journal of Otology Supplement* 15:9–13.

Washabaugh, W. 1979. Hearing and deaf signers on Providence Island. *Sign Language Studies* 24:191–214.

"We are not a quiet agency": ADWAS marks its first 10 years of helping victims become survivors. 1996. *Deaf Life,* March, pp. 10–11, 13–17.

Welsh, W. A. 1991. The economic impact of deafness. *Journal of the American Deafness and Rehabilitation Association* 24:72–80.

Wenokur, K. 1990. Mainstreaming vs. residential schools. *Deaf USA*, November, pp. 1, 4, 10, 23.

Whetter, D. 1989. Speaking with both hands in mouth. *Buff and Blue*, April 21, p. 4.

Wilcox, S., and S. Wilbers. 1987. The case for academic acceptance of American Sign Language. *Chronicle of Higher Education* 33 (42):30.

Wilson, J. 1973. *Introduction to social movements.* New York: Basic Books.

Woodward, J. 1973. Implicational lects on the deaf diglossic continuum. Ph.D. diss., Georgetown University, Washington, D.C.

———. 1974. Implicational variation in ASL: Negative incorporation. *Sign Language Studies* 5:20–30.

———. 1982. Beliefs about and attitudes toward deaf people and sign language on Providence Island. In *How you gonna get to heaven if you can't talk with Jesus: On depathologizing deafness,* edited by J. Woodward. Silver Spring, Md.: T. J. Publishers.

Woodward, J., and T. Allen. 1987. Classroom Use of ASL by Teachers. *Sign Language Studies* 54:1–10.

Woodward, J., T. Allen, and A. Schildroth. 1988. Linguistic and cultural role models for hearing-impaired children in elementary school programs. In *Language learning and deafness,* edited by M. Strong. Cambridge: Cambridge University Press.

Woolfolk Cross, D. 1989. Politics: The art of bamboozling. In *Exploring language,* edited by G. Goshgarian. 5th ed. Glenview, Ill.: Scott, Foresman and Company.

Index

Abused Deaf Women's Advocacy Services (ADWAS), 155
African Americans: Deaf, 107. *See also* Black English; Black Power movement; civil rights movement
Alexander Graham Bell Association for the Deaf, 24
American Association to Promote the Teaching of Speech to the Deaf, 24
American Sign Language (ASL): in Deaf education, 28–30, 76; and Deaf social movement, 9, 71; development of, 21–22; recognized at Gallaudet, 149; recognized as a language, 79–80, 92, 149, 156, 158–59; translation of, 15–16. *See also* Deaf Community, sign language as important to; Deaf social movement, language as issue for
Americans with Disabilities Act, 34, 94
Arensberg, C., 97n.2
argot, 79, 97–98n.4
Aristotle, 41
ASL. *See* American Sign Language
audism, 80–81

Bahan, Ben, 146, 150, 153, 157
Ballin, Albert, 57
Barnhart, J. S., 107–108
Bell, Alexander Graham, 23–25, 53–54, 156
Berger, Peter, 3
Bienvenu, MJ, 144
Biller, Moe, 122
Birnbaum, David, 110
Black English, 71, 72–73

Black Power movement, 9–10, 69–70, 108, 138–40, 160
Board of Education of the Hendrick Hudson Central School District v. Rowley, 86–87
Bonior, David, 124, 125
Bookman, Ann, 6
Bosmajian, Haig, 40, 41
Bourne, Bridgetta, 110, 118
Bravin, Philip, 100, 117, 119–20, 147
British National Union of the Deaf, 93
Brockriede, Wayne, 9, 139
Bryan, William Jennings, 65n.2
Burke, Kenneth, 126

California School for the Deaf, 34, 151
Campbell, K. K., 139
Carmichael, Stokely, 69, 83
Castle, Diane, 84–85
Castle, William C., 84
Cathcart, R. S., 135n.3
civil rights movement, 68–69, 82–83, 108
Clerc, Laurent, 21–23
cochlear implants, 143–45
Cogswell, Alice, 21, 59–60, 127, 135n.7
Cogswell, Mason Fitch, 21
communication policies, 149–51
consciousness-raising, 65n.5, 157
Contrucci, Victor, 148
Corson, Harvey, 111, 123, 135n.6, 157
court cases: relating to Deaf education, 86–87
Covell, Jerry, 110
Covington, V. C., 106
cultural diversity movements, 137–38, 139–40, 145, 149, 152, 156, 158, 173

193